A WORLD OF
FLAVOURS

A WORLD OF FLAVOURS

RECIPES FROM THE VOYAGES OF A MASTER CHEF

WILLI ELSENER
EXECUTIVE CHEF OF THE DORCHESTER, LONDON

With grateful thanks to my wife, Jayne Elsener
The Dorchester Management
Colin Webb, Publisher
John Midgley
Norma MacMillan
Caroline Davidson, Literary Agent
Sylvia Baumann, Elish Browning, Jamie Walker, Gilly Kings
Stuart Pate, Robert Gleeson
and all the other helping hands.

First published in Great Britain in 1995 by
Pavilion Books Limited
26 Upper Ground
London SE1 9PD

Text and recipes copyright © 1995 by Willi Elsener
The moral right of the author has been asserted

Food photography copyright © 1995 by James Murphy
Home Economist: Allyson Birch

Designed by Write Image

All rights reserved. No part of this publication may be reproduced, stored in a
retrieval system, or transmitted in any form or by any means, electronic,
mechanical, photocopying, recording, or otherwise, without the prior
permission of the copyright owner.

A CIP catalogue record for this book is available from the British Library

ISBN 1-85793-755 4

Printed and bound in Italy by Graphicom

2 4 6 8 10 9 7 5 3 1

This book may be ordered by post direct from the publisher. Please contact the
Marketing Department. But try your bookshop first.

Contents

6
Index of Recipes

8
Introduction

13
Cardamom

31
Turmeric

51
Chillies

65
Soy Sauce

83
Cinnamon

101
Sesame Oil

115
Limes

137
Coriander

159
Lemon Grass

173
Ginger

189
Basic Recipes

196
Index

200
Conversion Tables

RECIPES

FIRST COURSES

- 20 Caramelized onion and cottage cheese tart
- 22 Vegetable salad with warm tofu
- 36 Crunchy vegetable and goat's cheese salad
- 56 Oriental cucumber and salmon salad
- 57 Piquant pasta
- 60 Three-pepper mousse
- 72 Scallop salad, oriental-style
- 76 Broccoli and cauliflower timbale
- 80 Chicken salad with roasted garlic
- 109 Red mullet escabeche with samphire
- 109 Potted salmon and crab
- 120 Santen seafood salad
- 121 Deep-fried vegetables with a guacamole dip
- 125 Fillets of sole with roasted peppers
- 142 Chicken and French bean salad
- 144 Warm salmon timbale with asparagus
- 145 Salmon and pomelo parcel
- 165 Smoked halibut salad
- 165 Ham and papaya salad
- 180 Red mullet and eel terrine
- 184 Gingered prawn and melon salad
- 184 Cold marinated breast of chicken and vegetables

SOUPS

- 21 Cold melon soup with tapioca and mint
- 21 Red pepper and sweetcorn soup
- 37 Mussel and salmon soup
- 40 Aubergine soup
- 40 Creamed coconut and pumpkin soup
- 56 Spicy mushroom and chicken soup
- 81 Dublin Bay prawn broth
- 88 Celeriac and chestnut soup
- 89 Red lentil and clam soup
- 124 Lime-flavoured chicken and noodle soup
- 124 Chilled crab and cucumber soup
- 142 Sweet potato and coriander soup
- 143 Shiitake and smoked haddock soup
- 143 Mango and chicken soup
- 164 Prawn and salmon soup

FISH AND SHELLFISH

- 23 Salmon eastern-style
- 41 Fillet of sea bass with Indian spices
- 42 Oven-baked aubergine and smoked mackerel
- 57 Prawn and sweetcorn chilli
- 61 Fillet of sea bream with shiitake mushrooms
- 81 Salmon steak with celery and cashew nuts
- 73 Red mullet with black beans and mashed potatoes
- 77 Barbecued monkfish and prawns with aubergines and plum tomatoes
- 91 Monkfish with beansprouts and mangetout
- 108 Baked salmon in lotus leaves
- 112 Fillet of sea bass with Chinese greens and bacon
- 126 Grilled tuna steak with a virgin olive oil and garlic sauce
- 127 Lime-crusted fillet of brill
- 127 Smoked mackerel gratin
- 132 Mackerel with peri-peri sauce
- 132 Baked sea bream with asparagus in a lime sauce

148	Sea bream served on an aubergine purée	186	Lamb casserole with stem ginger and cashew nuts
156	Cod steak with tomato salsa		
156	Red mullet and monkfish stew		**Desserts and Cakes**
157	Prawns and okra with coriander	29	Mango gâteau
157	Gratinated coriander mussels	30	Banana crumble with passion fruit and coconut
168	Scallops and prawns with a glazed potato crown	30	Cardamom-flavoured peach gratin
181	Steamed red snapper	49	Pumpkin and cashew nut cake
185	Salmon roulade served with soya beansprouts	50	Apricot crumble
		96	Ricotta cheesecake
	Meat and Poultry	97	Cinnamon and fig gratin
24	Roast quail with nectarine	100	Pumpkin and coconut cake
25	Cardamom rice with chicken and fish	100	Poached pear with cinnamon
28	Roast guinea fowl with kumquat sauce	136	Peach and mascarpone mousse
43	Tropical mango chicken	186	Sticky banana pudding
44	Honey chicken thighs	187	Ginger and coconut tart
44	Braised turmeric chicken	187	Baked gingered apples
45	Steak with sweet potato sauce	188	Stem ginger and pear cake
45	Medallions of lamb with a turmeric crust		
48	Peppers filled with minced lamb		**Basic Recipes**
61	Sirloin steak with a black olive sauce	189	Mamdouh's rice
64	Roast marinated guinea fowl	190	Black bean sauce
64	Old-fashioned pork stroganoff	190	Fish stock
82	Barbecued sirloin steak with horseradish relish	190	Chicken stock
82	Creamy glazed chicken legs	191	Brown chicken stock
90	Tomato bredie	191	Brown veal stock
90	Lamb and okra hotpot	192	Veal glace
92	Chicken with cinnamon sauce	192	Lamb stock
93	Roast pheasant with apple and papaya	192	Brown lamb stock
113	Chicken kebabs	193	Vegetable stock
114	Roasted sesame chicken	193	Curry sauce for fish
128	Lamb chops with limed apricot confit	193	Mashed potatoes
129	Medallions of pork in lime sauce	194	Roast potatoes
133	Lime chicken with mushrooms	194	Orange sauce
149	Stuffed chicken breast wrapped in Parma ham	194	Chocolate sauce
152	Loin of lamb wrapped in a mousse of coriander and bread croutons	194	Raspberry sauce
153	Pork steak with glazed goat's cheese	195	Sauce anglaise
158	Roast duck with banana and orange sauce	195	Vanilla sponge
169	Tangy guinea fowl with sweetcorn chutney	195	Sweet pastry
172	Loin of rabbit and braised lentils	195	Shortcrust pastry

Introduction

The smells, the sights and the mouthwatering tastes of the kitchen have been part of my life for as long as I can remember. My earliest memories are those from our family hotel and, in particular, the kitchen where my grandfather and mother bustled about. This warm haven of activity – and the delicious morsels that came my way – bred in me a life-long love of cooking.

In my infancy the kitchen offered the warmth of security. In my childhood it was a retreat from the playground, where pangs of hunger were quickly dispersed by the tasty offerings of that day. Without much effort I became something of a gourmet, knowing more about the intimacies of the kitchen than of my multiplication tables! The kitchen was a constant source of pleasure.

My apprenticeship put an end to that! Suddenly cooking came to mean hours of hard work, endless days of peeling vegetables, making stocks and cleaning pots. None of this, however, diminished my love of cooking. For at the end of it all, there was always delicious food on offer to our guests.

At this stage my vision of cooking was restricted to the traditional and precise ways of the Swiss kitchens in which I had worked. My thirst for knowledge was hampered by a Chef who, although well travelled and knowledgeable on the cuisines of other countries (he had, for example, worked for the King of Addis Ababa), kept his prize recipes under lock and key!

Being young and adventurous, I was not content with this, and at the earliest opportunity I took the plunge and travelled abroad. Since then, the excitement of discovering new places and returning to old favourites has remained with me.

For many years, I worked in hotels that were 'seasonal'. This meant that I would work for about eight months of the year, and then have the remaining months to travel.

My journeys – often with limited resources and working to make ends meet – have stretched from Japan across Asia, touching on Africa and across to South America. Having the opportunity on occasion to spend three months in one country opened up a whole new world. I discovered different cultures and met all kinds of people – the most interesting being the least sophisticated. Often it was while sharing a modest meal with a native family, or sitting on a racketing train surrounded by livestock, that I learnt the most.

'Going native' meant that I saw sights often missed by the tourist, and sampled food not yet adapted to the European palate. I explored local markets with relish and discovered a wealth of new ingredients. A dream for a chef!

Although my culinary background is firmly rooted in European tradition, my personal style of cooking has been much influenced by these journeys all over the world. They have given me a wealth of knowledge far beyond any that could be found in a book. My travels have become inextricably intertwined with my love of food.

Today, after 20 years of training and travelling, I have reached a destination – The Dorchester Hotel, London, where I have the good fortune to be Executive Chef. However, my urge to travel and learn has not diminished, and I am resigned to being a life-long student.

Between 1988 and 1990, the hotel closed for major refurbishment. During this time I was instrumental in designing the new kitchens and formulating the food concepts for our new restaurants. The knowledge gained from years of travelling undoubtedly stood me in good stead.

Today, in our seven kitchens, over 110 chefs prepare an amazing repertoire of food: French, Italian, Chinese, Japanese, Malaysian, Arabic and, naturally, British. Managing this means that, at work, cooking takes on a totally different perspective.

My position now bears little resemblance to that for which I originally trained. It involves incredibly long hours and lots of hard work, and is constantly changing. It is challenging. It is frustrating at times. But, above all, it is rewarding. That is what keeps me motivated.

On a personal level, cooking – like travelling – is a relaxing hobby. Here I enjoy experimenting with ingredients, combining them to produce dishes with new textures and sometimes unexpected flavours. For me there is no activity more rewarding, and few that can be such fun, as sharing with family and friends a lovingly prepared and carefully presented meal. In this book I want to share this enjoyment with you.

Years back, many of the ingredients I encountered on my journeys were virtually unknown in European kitchens. Today, we can happily buy most of them off the supermarket shelf. For this book I chose ten such ingredients that I consider to be important, and incorporated them in simple, appetizing and colourful dishes.

Each ingredient opened up a whole new world of flavours for me, a spectrum of taste. For a chef, unravelling the secrets of these spices, herbs and other flavourings has been exciting – an adventure. Each evokes so many memories. I am, therefore, not only presenting you with a collection of recipes, but also with some of my experiences while travelling and the people I've met who have enriched my cooking and my life. In addition, I offer some of the hints and tips that I picked up along the way.

Introduction

This collection of recipes has evolved over many years. Some are old, others new. Some have been developed in The Dorchester kitchens for unique occasions, others more simply in my kitchen at home. Some have started as a sketch after a stimulating day in a busy street market, others are the result of a lingering mixture of aromas or an unforgettable taste. Others still have evolved by sheer mistake, and some from the cooking of friends. Each is a personal favourite. All have been tested twice over.

I hope the recipes will excite and intrigue you. All are aimed at the enthusiastic home cook, cooking at home to please family and friends. Most of the ingredients are easily obtainable – for those that may be a little more exotic, I suggest where you can find them. Methods are written simply step-by-step and are easy to follow. For the more health conscious, or for those of us watching our waistlines, all recipes also give approximate calorie content.

This book offers a glimpse of how everyday food can be transformed with the help of new and often unexpected flavours. I hope it will encourage you to venture even further on your own, to transform a love of good food into a daily habit.

WILLI ELSENER
1995.

Cardamom

CARDAMOM IS AMONGST THE OLDEST AND MOST HIGHLY PRIZED SPICES IN THE WORLD. FROM THE RAIN FORESTS OF SOUTHERN INDIA AND SRI LANKA IT WAS BARTERED ALONG THE ANCIENT CARAVAN ROUTES UNTIL IT EVENTUALLY REACHED EUROPE. TODAY CARDAMOM IS CULTIVATED IN ITS NATIVE HABITAT AS WELL AS IN VIETNAM, GUATEMALA AND TANZANIA. IT IS THE THIRD MOST EXPENSIVE SPICE AFTER SAFFRON AND VANILLA, AND IS EASILY FOUND IN ITS VARIOUS FORMS ON ANY SPICE RACK.

Like most cooks I used to use cardamom powder without a second thought. My real discovery of this spice, however, came one day as I walked around a small village up in Jaffna. Along both sides of the native road, which had been worn out over the years by the wooden wheels of the carts pulled along by oxen, I saw what looked to me like washing lines covered with huge leaves. I could not figure out what these were, and there appeared to be no one to ask. Walking a few yards further along the road, I looked over a low wooden fence made out of small wooden twigs, simply tied together with strings made from the coconut tree, and caught sight of an old woman sitting on the ground rolling the leaves. As she lifted her tanned head towards me, I saw that in her mouth she had a cigar. It was quite unusual for me to see a woman smoking a cigar, but I learnt that this is common in some parts of Asia. We started talking to each other, and she showed me how to roll the leaves on a flat smooth piece of stone that acted as a work table where she must have rolled thousands of cigars, and to tighten them with a piece of fine red string that she turned quickly around the leaves to keep the cigar in shape. She made me try to roll my own cigar, but my hands did not have the skill she had acquired. My cigar looked like a bunch of squashed leaves. She looked at it, looked into my eyes and had a good giggle, hiding her few remaining teeth with her flat hand. It did not matter that I was not able to make the right shaped cigar. Talking to her was the fulfilment of the day.

Suddenly she stood up, went to a nearby hut and came back with a cup of tea to show her hospitality. However, it was not like normal tea but had a tremendously refreshing flavour and some bits and pieces floating in it. I was a little suspicious and asked the old woman what they were. She went again into the hut and came back holding in her wrinkled, shaking hand a woven wooden basket with some hard greenish pods in it. She peeled the skin off one of the pods and gave me the dark seeds inside, indicating that I should chew them. The aroma was mellow, but what a lingering, penetrating and refreshing taste! She told me these were cardamom and that she used them in her cooking everyday.

I was suddenly aware that while we had been talking nearly the whole village had gathered around us to check out the stranger who had invaded the old woman's privacy. A stranger in the village was a very rare thing, and they welcomed me warmly.

Later I was taken by one of the villagers, followed by the old woman, to see the large cardamom bushes – about 2-4m/6-12 ft in maturity. These bore small oval 'fruits' after flowering, which were harvested just before opening and then dried. Since then I have encountered cardamom in many places and continue to learn of its versatility.

Cardamom can enhance both savoury and sweet tastes. It is widely used in the preparation of many meat and fish dishes; it adds a sharp bitterness to soups and rice too. It is equally agreeable in breads, cakes, pastries and puddings – even in ice cream – and is one of the main components of garam masala and curry powders. Cardamom can be used to flavour bitters and spirits as well as warm drinks, such as my 'tea'. I have since learnt from my Egyptian chef, Mamdouh Kamal Abbas, that in the Middle East the particular flavour of cardamom is prized in coffee, and up to 50% of the spice is mixed with coffee beans.

Cardamom is used outside the kitchen as a remedy for stomach disorders. Its essential oil is used in perfumes; and chewing on a few seeds is the perfect breath cleanser.

CARDAMOM

Caramelized Onion and Cottage Cheese Tart (page 20)

Caramelized onion and cottage cheese tart

Serves 4

150g/5 oz shortcrust pastry (see basic recipe, page 195)
flour to dust dough
1 egg, lightly beaten with a fork
1 tbsp vegetable oil
3 whole cardamom pods
250 g/9 oz onions, peeled and thinly sliced
25 g/1 oz caster sugar (2 tbsp granulated sugar)
100 ml/4 fl oz red wine
salt and freshly ground black pepper
100 g/4 oz (½ cup) cottage cheese
150 ml/5 fl oz double cream (heavy cream)
mixed salad leaves, such as radicchio, curly endive (frisée), chicory (Belgian endive), rocket (arugula)
fresh chervil and dill, to garnish

Dressing

2 tbsp red wine vinegar
1 pinch of English mustard powder
5 tbsp sunflower oil

You will need

4 flan tins or loose-based tartlet moulds, each 10 cm/4 inches diameter and 1 cm/½ inch deep

Oven temperature

190°C/375°F/Gas mark 5

(Approximately 650 calories per portion)

Ideal as a first course or light meal, this delicious combination of onion and cheese in small tartlet cases is served warm on a bed of fresh salad. The tartlets can be cooked a couple of hours before serving and simply reheated in the oven when required.

Pastry cases

Prepare the shortcrust pastry according to the basic recipe and then leave to rest for at least 30 minutes in the refrigerator. Grease the flan tins (or use non-stick ones).

Lightly dust the pastry dough with flour and roll it out to about 3 mm/⅛ inch thick. Using a round cutter or knife, cut out 4 discs at least 1 cm/½ inch wider than the flan tins. Press the discs lightly into the greased flan tins, then line with greaseproof paper (wax paper) and fill with dried beans. Bake blind in the lower part of the preheated oven for about 10 minutes.

Take the pastry cases out of the oven and remove the paper and beans. Brush each case with a little of the beaten egg and return to the oven to bake for a further 5 minutes. (This will seal the pastry and prevent the cases becoming soggy when the filling is added.) Remove the tartlet cases from the oven and keep aside.

Filling

Heat the vegetable oil in a non-stick pan. Add the cardamom pods and cook until they are golden brown. Reduce the heat. Add the sliced onion and sweat until translucent, without colouring. Now add the sugar and cook for a further minute or two or until it starts to caramelize slightly. When this happens, add the red wine and stir well, then simmer on a low heat until the liquid has fully evaporated. Do not forget to stir or it may catch and burn. Remove from the heat and season. Allow to cool, then remove the cardamom pods.

Divide the onion mixture among the four tartlet cases, then divide the cottage cheese and place it in a dollop in the centre of each tart, on top of the onion confit. Mix together the cream and the beaten egg remaining from brushing the tartlet cases. Season with salt and pepper. Pour this mixture into the tartlet cases. Bake in the preheated oven for 20–25 minutes or until the filling is set and golden brown. (If you are left with any of the egg mixture, it will make a small amount of scrambled egg.)

Dressing

Whilst the tartlets are baking, wash the salad leaves and prepare the dressing. To do this, simply mix all the ingredients together. (I find the easiest way is to put everything into a small bottle, screw the lid on tightly and then give it a good shake.)

To Finish

When the tartlets are cooked, remove them from the oven and allow them to rest for about 5 minutes. Meanwhile, toss the salad leaves in the dressing and arrange on 4 plates. Then carefully remove each tartlet from its flan tin and place it in the centre of the salad. To add a final touch, garnish with a few fresh herbs.

Cold melon soup with tapioca and mint

(Approximately 190 calories per portion)

This is a lovely refreshing soup, especially good during the summer months. If you find the soup is not sweet enough, shake a little icing sugar (confectioners' sugar) into it through a fine sieve.

Bring a saucepan of salted water to the boil. Add the tapioca and cook until tender. Allow it to cool, then drain and keep to one side.

Mix together the port and white wines in a saucepan. Add the cardamom pods and slowly bring to the boil. Simmer gently for 2 minutes, then remove from the heat and allow to cool. Strain through a fine sieve into a large bowl and keep aside.

Cut the melons in half and remove the seeds. Cut about 2 tbsp of the flesh into small dice shapes and keep to one side for the garnish. Remove the remaining flesh from the skin and cut roughly into chunks. Add to the bowl of cooled wine and marinate for 2 hours. Using a hand blender or food processor, purée until smooth. Pass through a sieve back into a bowl and add the cream. Then gently stir in the cooked tapioca pearls. Place the mixture in the refrigerator and chill until ice cold. Alternatively, set the bowl in a larger bowl containing crushed ice. Keep ice cold until serving.

To Finish

When ready to serve, remove from the refrigerator, add the chopped mint, the mineral water and the 2 tbsp of diced melon flesh. Pour into chilled soup cups, garnish with mint sprigs and serve.

Serves 4

75 g/3 oz (1/2 cup) tapioca
40 ml/1 1/2 fl oz port wine
100 ml/4 fl oz dry white wine
5 whole cardamom pods
2 ripe ogen or other small green-fleshed melons
100 ml/4 fl oz single cream (light cream)
1/2 tsp chopped fresh mint
50 ml/2 fl oz sparking mineral water
sprigs of mint, to garnish

Red pepper and sweetcorn soup

(Approximately 160 calories per portion)

After a fascinating day in the ruins of Machu Picchu in the Andes, a heavenly smell of corn on the cob drew me to a native trader. He offered me an ear of sweetcorn, which I ate with relish, regardless of the rusty cooking pot from which it came.
The concentrated smell of sweetcorn remained with me and inspired this recipe.

Start by toasting the cardamom. To do this, simply place them on an oven tray and pop them under the grill (broiler) to brown. Do watch them carefully as you don't want them to burn. Then allow to cool slightly and wrap them in a piece of clean muslin or cheesecloth. Keep to one side until needed.

Cut the corn kernels from the cobs using a sharp knife. Reserve the cobs. Bring a saucepan of water to the boil – do not add any salt as this will toughen the corn – then add the kernels and boil for 3–5 minutes or until cooked. Drain and plunge immediately into a bowl of iced water. Drain and keep aside.

Heat the vegetable oil in a saucepan. Add the sugar, red peppers, onion and garlic and sweat for 3–4 minutes on a medium heat without colouring. Add the corn cobs and the cardamom bag. Add the chicken stock and bring slowly to the boil. Reduce the heat, cover with a lid and simmer for about 20 minutes.

Remove the cobs and cardamom bag, and purée the mixture using a hand blender or food processor. Return the soup to the saucepan and bring back to the boil.

Serves 4

5 whole cardamom pods
2 fresh ears of sweetcorn
2 tbsp vegetable oil
1 tsp sugar
2 red sweet peppers, seeds removed, coarsely diced
1 onion, peeled and finely chopped
1 garlic clove, peeled and finely chopped
750 ml/1 1/4 pt (3 cups) chicken stock (see basic recipe, page 190)
1/2 lemon, juiced
salt and freshly ground pepper

To Finish

Add the corn kernels and lemon juice, heat through and season with salt and freshly ground pepper. Serve hot.

Vegetable salad with warm tofu

(Approximately 295 calories per portion)

Although familiar with tofu, it was only after my work experience in Japan, where tofu is commonly used, that I started to experiment with it. Made from soya milk, tofu has a slightly nutty flavour, is full of vegetable protein and is incredibly versatile.

Different types are available, but for this recipe I use the pressed, firmer type which is readily available in large supermarkets or in Japanese or Chinese shops. It's easy to cut, and acts like a sponge, so it will absorb and retain the magical flavours of the salad dressing until it's enjoyed by you.

Serves 2

- 75 g/3 oz of any salad leaves in season, such as curly endive (frisée), radicchio, mâche, spinach, etc
- 1 spring onion (green onion), cut into 3 mm / 1/8 inch rings
- 50 g/2 oz (1/2 cup) soya beansprouts, heads removed
- 50 g/2 oz (1/2 cup) mixed sprouts from other beans and seeds
- 200 g/7 oz French or other green beans, topped and tailed
- 1 small carrot, peeled and cut into 3 mm/1/8 inch slices
- 100 g/4 oz pressed tofu
- 1 tbsp flour
- 2 tbsp vegetable oil

Dressing
- 1 tsp clear honey
- 1 tbsp sherry vinegar
- 2 tbsp walnut oil
- salt and freshly ground white pepper to taste
- 1 pinch of freshly ground cardamom
- 1/2 tsp chopped fresh chives

Salad

Wash the salad leaves and prepare the spring onion and beansprouts. Place in a large bowl.

Bring a pan of salted water to the boil, add the beans and cook for about 2 minutes - keep them crisp. Have ready a bowl of iced water. Drain the beans (reserving 1 tbsp of the cooking liquid for the dressing) and immediately plunge the beans into the iced water. This will stop the cooking process and ensure that they stay nice and crisp. Repeat this process with the carrots, but only allow them to cook for about 30 seconds. When the beans and carrots are cold, drain them and add them to the salad leaves.

Dressing

While the beans and carrots are cooling, prepare the dressing. Dissolve the honey in the cooking liquid reserved from the beans, then allow it to cool. Add all the other dressing ingredients and whisk together. Keep aside.

To Finish

Cut the tofu into 1 cm / 1/2 inch dice, season with salt and pepper and dust with flour. (I find the easiest way to do this is to put the flour into a plastic bag, add the diced tofu and shake it about.) Heat the oil in a frying pan and fry the tofu pieces until golden brown. Remove them from the pan and keep warm.

To serve, toss the salad leaves and vegetables together in the dressing, then divide between 2 plates. Sprinkle the warm tofu on top and serve immediately.

Salmon Eastern-Style

(Approximately 560 calories per portion)

A unique dish, full of flavour, this uses a Chinese mushroom that is known as cloud ear, wood ear or tree ear. Widely used in Chinese cooking, the mushroom has a pleasant but not too strong flavour. Ear mushrooms can be bought in Chinese supermarkets. If you are not lucky enough to be able to buy them fresh, dried ones can be used instead. Soak these overnight and rinse thoroughly before using.

Infusion
Toast the cardamom pods under the grill (broiler) until golden brown. Remove and allow to cool, then wrap the cardamom pods, orange zest, star anise and fennel stalk in a piece of muslin or cheesecloth and tie together with string like a money bag. Put into a saucepan, add the fish stock and bring to the boil. Simmer gently for 10 minutes, skimming off any impurities as necessary. Remove the muslin bag and keep the infusion for the sauce.

Fish
Heat the vegetable oil in a non-stick frying pan. Season the salmon fillets with salt and freshly ground pepper and place in the pan, browning quickly on both sides. Remove the salmon from the pan and keep aside.

Sauce
In the meantime, heat the vegetable oil in a saucepan, add the chopped chilli, ginger and ear mushrooms and sweat for about 30 seconds, without colouring. Add the sugar followed by the oyster sauce. Finally, add the infusion prepared earlier and bring to the boil. Adjust the seasoning as necessary.

To Finish
Pass the sauce through a sieve into a bowl. Remove the chilli, ginger and mushroom from the sieve and put into an ovenproof dish. Set the salmon on top and then pour the sauce over the salmon. Arrange the 6 ear mushrooms around the fish. Cover with a lid and bake in the preheated oven for 8–10 minutes or until cooked but still moist. Garnish with the spring onion and herbs and serve immediately.

Serves 2

2 tbsp vegetable oil
2 salmon fillets, skin removed, each 150 g/5 oz
salt and freshly ground pepper
6 fresh ear mushrooms

Infusion

10 whole cardamom pods
1 piece of orange zest, 5 cm/2 inches long
1 piece of star anise
1 piece of dried fennel stalk, 2.5 cm/1 inch long, or you can substitute a piece of fresh bulb fennel
200 ml/7 fl oz fish stock (see basic recipe, page 190)

Sauce

1 tbsp vegetable oil
½ tsp finely chopped fresh hot red chilli pepper (seeded)
1 tsp peeled fresh ginger cut into fine strips
6 tbsp ear mushrooms cut into fine strips
½ tsp caster sugar (granulated sugar)
1 tbsp oyster sauce

Garnish

1 spring onion (green onion), green leaves removed, cut into fine strips
fresh coriander leaves (cilantro) and dill

Oven temperature

180°C/350°F/Gas mark 4

Roast Quail with Nectarine

Serves 2

1 tbsp vegetable oil
2 quails, cleaned
salt and freshly ground pepper
1 ripe nectarine
rosemary sprigs, to garnish (optional)

Sauce

1 tbsp caster sugar (granulated sugar)
1 tbsp water
1 lime, juiced
2 whole cardamom pods
100 ml/4 fl oz brown chicken stock (see basic recipe, page 191)
½ tbsp cornflour (cornstarch)
50 ml/2 fl oz sherry
½ tsp finely chopped fresh rosemary

Oven temperature

180°C/350°F/Gas mark 4

(Approximately 220 calories per portion)

To prepare the sauce for this recipe, you'll need to caramelize the sugar. To do this, follow my instructions carefully. Do not allow the sugar to brown too much or the resultant sauce will be bitter.

QUAILS

Heat the oil in a roasting pan in the preheated oven. Season the quails with salt and freshly ground pepper and place them in the pan. Brown them quickly on both sides in the oven, then leave to roast for about 12 minutes or until medium cooked and tender.

NECTARINE

Preparing the nectarine. Place it in boiling water for 30 seconds, then immediately plunge into a bowl of iced water. Drain and peel – the skin will slide off quite easily. Cut half the nectarine into dice shapes and keep aside. The other half is not used in this recipe – so enjoy it now!

SAUCE

Heat the sugar in a saucepan on a medium heat for a few minutes until golden brown. Do not stir! Remove from the heat immediately and allow it to cool for 5 minutes. Then add the water, lime juice and cardamom pods. Place back over the heat until the sugar has dissolved, then bring to the boil. Add the chicken stock and boil for a further 5 minutes. Mix the cornflour with the Sherry. Add a little of the hot sauce to it, then whisk into the sauce in the pan. Simmer until thickened. Pass through a sieve into a clean saucepan.

TO FINISH

When the quails are cooked, remove them from the oven and allow them to rest for 5 minutes.

Meanwhile, bring the sauce back to the boil. Add the diced nectarine and simmer for a minute. Add the rosemary and season.

Cut each quail in half, and place the 4 halves in a serving dish. Pour the sauce over, garnish with rosemary sprigs and serve.

Cardamom rice with chicken and fish

(Approximately 340 calories per portion)

A one-pot dish full of flavour, colour and texture, this is enhanced by a technique I learnt from my Egyptian chef, Mamdouh Kamal Abbas. He always toasts cardamom pods under the grill until golden brown, to strengthen their flavour and add a slight nuttiness.

Rice

Start by toasting the cardamom. To do this, simply place them on an oven tray and pop them under the grill (broiler) to brown. Do watch them carefully as you don't want them to burn. Then allow to cool slightly and wrap them in a piece of clean muslin or cheesecloth. Keep to one side until needed.

Heat the olive oil in a non-stick frying pan. Add the shallot and garlic and sweat until translucent, without colouring. Then add the peppers and sweat for a further minute. Add the prepared cardamom bag. Pour in the white wine and bring to the boil. Transfer the mixture to a flameproof dish with a lid. Add the rice and bay leaf. Heat the chicken stock to boiling and add this too. Season with salt and freshly ground white pepper and bring back to the boil. Cover with a lid and place in the lower part of the preheated oven to cook for 16 minutes.

Chicken and Fish

Whilst the rice is cooking, prepare the chicken and fish. Using the same frying pan as before, heat the 2 tbsp of oil in it. Season the chicken with salt and freshly ground white pepper and brown in the pan for a few seconds. Then reduce the heat and pan-fry until nearly cooked. Remove and keep to one side. Using the same pan, lightly brown the sole strips. Remove and keep together with the chicken. Season the king prawns and brown them lightly. Place these with the chicken and sole, cover and keep warm.

To Finish

Remove the rice from the oven and taste to check that it is cooked but still moist. If not, return to the oven for a few more minutes. When cooked, gently mix in the chicken, sole and king prawns. Cover the dish and leave (outside the oven) for a further 5 minutes to heat through. Then stir in the diced tomato using a fork and season to taste. Remove the bay leaf and cardamom bag. Sprinkle with spring onions and serve.

Serves 4

- 2 tbsp olive oil
- 2 skinless boneless chicken breasts (breast halves), cut into 1 cm/½ inch cubes
- 120 g/4 oz sole fillets, cut into finger-sized strips
- 8 raw king prawns (large shrimp), peeled, deveined and heads removed
- 1 medium-sized tomato, peeled, seeded and diced
- 1 spring onion (green onion), cut into fine rings

Rice

- 20 whole cardamom pods
- 1 tbsp olive oil
- 1 shallot, peeled and chopped
- ½ garlic clove, peeled and crushed with a knife or garlic press
- 1 green sweet pepper, seeds removed, cut into 5 mm/¼ inch cubes
- 1 red sweet pepper, seeds removed, cut into 5 mm/¼ inch cubes
- 2 tbsp white wine
- 150 g/5 oz (¼ cup + 2 tbsp) long-grain rice
- ¼ bay leaf
- 450 ml/15 fl oz chicken stock (see basic recipe, page 190)
- salt and freshly ground white pepper

Oven temperature

170°C/325°F/Gas mark 3

A WORLD OF FLAVOURS

*C*ardamom Rice
with Chicken and
Fish (page 25)

Roast guinea fowl with kumquat sauce

Serves 4

4 guinea fowl breasts (breast halves)
salt and freshly ground pepper
1 tbsp vegetable oil
3 whole cardamom pods

Sauce

6 fresh kumquats
2 oranges, juiced
4 tsp Grand Marnier liqueur
250 ml/8 fl oz brown chicken stock (see basic recipe, page 191)
2 tsp cornflour (cornstarch)

Oven temperature

180°C/350°F/Gas mark 4

(Approximately 220 calories per portion)

Kumquats are a small fruit that I have encountered in many parts of the world, but which originated in China. They look like a mini-mini orange. The thin skin is edible and the flavour pleasantly sharp. This complements the richness of guinea fowl perfectly.

Kumquats

Cut the kumquats into 3 mm/$\frac{1}{8}$ inch slices and remove the seeds. Cook in boiling salted water for 20 seconds and refresh by plunging immediately into a bowl of iced water. When cold, drain them and keep to one side for the sauce.

Guinea fowl breasts

Prepare the guinea fowl breasts by trimming off any excess fat from the edges, then season with salt and pepper.

Heat the oil in a frying pan and add the cardamom pods. Push the pods to one side and add the guinea fowl breasts, skin side down first. Pan-fry until brown and crispy. Then turn over and seal the other side. Remove from the pan to an oven tray and cook in the preheated oven for about 10 minutes. Remove the breasts from the oven tray and allow to rest in a warm place for approximately 5 minutes.

Sauce

Whilst the guinea fowl breasts are in the oven, prepare the sauce. Using the same frying pan as before, drain off the oil but retain the cardamom pods. With the pods back in the pan, add the orange juice and the Grand Marnier. Bring to the boil and simmer gently to reduce to half of the quantity. Add the brown chicken stock and bring back to the boil. Pass the sauce through a fine chinois or a sieve lined with muslin or cheesecloth into a saucepan. Bring to the boil again. Add the kumquat slices. In a small bowl mix the cornflour with 2 tbsp of cold water. Add a little of the boiling sauce to it, and then whisk it all into the sauce in the pan. Bring back to the boil and cook until thickened. Season with salt and freshly ground pepper.

To Finish

When the breasts are ready, place them in a serving dish and pour over the sauce.

Mango Gâteau

(Approximately 465 calories per portion)

To ensure that the gâteau is full of flavour, choose mangoes that are at their peak and well ripened.

BASE
Cut the vanilla sponge horizontally to make a layer about 5 mm/¼ inch thick. Place this in the cake pan and keep aside. The remainder of the cake will not be used in this recipe, so is ideal for freezing for use in another gâteau or perhaps a trifle at a later date.

MANGO
Peel the mangoes with a knife, then cut the flesh lengthwise away from the large stone in the centre. Cut the flesh from 2 of the mangoes into coarse cubes and keep aside. Cut the flesh from the third mango into small dices and keep separately for folding into the mousse.

SYRUP
Place the water and sugar in a saucepan. Gently heat until all the sugar has dissolved. Simmer for 2 minutes. Allow to cool and keep aside.

MOUSSE
Toast the cardamom pods under the grill (broiler) until golden brown. Mix together the sugar, cardamom pods and the coarse cubes of flesh from the 2 mangoes in a saucepan. Heat gently until the sugar has dissolved. Simmer for 4 minutes. Remove the cardamom pods. Purée the mixture and pass through a sieve back into the saucepan. Return to simmering point, then remove from the heat. Immediately sprinkle over the gelatine and whisk in to dissolve completely. Stir in the lemon juice. Allow to cool (not in the refrigerator), but not to set.

Whip the cream until soft peaks form, then fold into the cool fruit purée, using a rubber spatula. Gently fold in the diced mango flesh. Using a perfectly clean bowl, whisk the egg whites until stiff, then fold into the mixture.

Brush the sponge layer with the prepared sugar syrup. Pour the mousse on to the centre of the sponge and use a spatula to spread it evenly. Cover with plastic film and allow to set in the refrigerator for 3–4 hours.

TO FINISH
Using a knife, loosen the gâteau from the side of the pan, cutting all around as close as possible to the pan. Gently remove the side of the pan and the loose base. Place the gâteau on a plate.

Decorate with whipped cream, raspberries and mint.

Serves 6

Base
1 bought or home-made vanilla sponge cake round, 18 cm/7 inches in diameter (see basic recipe, page 195)

Mousse
3 fresh, ripe mangoes
12 whole cardamom pods
1 tsp caster sugar (granulated sugar)
1 tbsp (6 g) unflavoured gelatine powder
¼ tsp lemon juice
250 ml/8 fl oz double cream (heavy cream)
2 egg whites

Syrup
6 tbsp water
3 tbsp caster sugar (granulated sugar)

Garnish
100 ml/4 fl oz double cream (heavy cream), whipped
6 raspberries
6 sprigs of mint

You will need
a round loose-bottomed cake pan, 18 cm/7 inches in diameter

Banana Crumble with Passion Fruit and Coconut

Serves 2

100 ml/4 fl oz fresh orange juice, strained
6 whole cardamom pods
1 passion fruit
2 large ripe bananas
2 tbsp dry brioche crumbs
1 tbsp brown sugar
½ tsp ground cinnamon
1 ½ tbsp desiccated coconut (unsweetened dried shredded coconut)
passion fruit sorbet or ice cream (optional)

Oven temperature
180°C/350°F/Gas mark 4

Grill (broiler)
very hot

(Approximately 185 calories per portion)

A quick and easy dessert, serve this with an ice-cream or thick cream.

Place the orange juice in a saucepan and add the cardamom pods. Bring to the boil and simmer gently for 3 minutes. Remove from the heat and allow to cool. Remove the cardamom pods. Cut the passion fruit in half, scoop out flesh and mix with the orange juice. Keep aside. Peel the bananas and cut into 5 mm/¼ inch thick slices. Arrange these in concentric rings in a small ovenproof dish. Pour the cold orange and passion fruit mixture over the bananas and keep aside.

Lightly mix the brioche crumbs with the brown sugar, cinnamon powder and desiccated coconut. Sprinkle this evenly over the sliced bananas.

To Finish

Bake in the preheated oven for about 5 minutes, then place under the preheated grill until golden brown. Serve hot, with sorbet or ice-cream if you like.

Cardamom-Flavoured Peach Gratin

Serves 4

6 large, ripe yet firm peaches
200 g/7 oz caster sugar (1 cup granulated sugar)
250 ml/8 fl oz fresh orange juice
8 whole cardamom pods

Gratin mixture

4 egg yolks (freeze the egg whites for another dish)
2 tbsp sugar
4 tbsp single cream (light cream)
1 tbsp peach liqueur
½ tsp grated lemon zest

Garnish

icing sugar (confectioners' sugar)
nice ripe raspberries
fresh mint

You will need
4 individual shallow flameproof dishes or plates

Grill (broiler)
medium–high

(Approximately 210 calories per portion)

When preparing the gratin mixture, it will be quite 'runny', but through whisking, and from the heat generated by the water, it will gradually thicken. Keep a constant eye on the temperature of the water: it needs to remain just below simmering point. When you are able to 'draw' a ribbon across the top of the mixture, it has reached the correct consistency.

Peaches

Wash the peaches, then drop them into a pan of boiling water. Blanch for about 30 seconds. Using a slotted spoon, take them out and place in a bowl of iced water. When cold, drain the peaches and carefully remove the skin with a knife. Cut each peach into 8 wedges (discard the stones) and place in a bowl. Keep aside.

Combine the sugar, orange juice and cardamom pods in a saucepan. Heat gently, without stirring until the sugar has dissolved, then bring to the boil and boil for about 3 minutes. Add the peach wedges, return to the boil and then remove from the heat. Cover with a lid and allow to cool.

Drain the syrup carefully from the peach wedges. Gently pat them dry with paper towels, then arrange them in the flameproof dishes, in a ring. Keep aside. (The syrup is not required again in this recipe, but would be delicious used in your next fresh fruit salad.)

Gratin Mixture

This needs to be made at the last minute, so when you are ready mix all the gratin ingredients together in a metal bowl using a whisk. Set the bowl over a pan of almost simmering water and continue whisking until the mixture is thick and foamy. It is important that it not be too 'runny'. Pour over the peaches.

To Finish

Place the dish under the preheated grill until golden brown. Using a fine sieve, dust icing sugar over the surface. Decorate with raspberries and mint and serve.

Turmeric

TURMERIC IS A PERENNIAL TROPICAL PLANT BELONGING TO THE GINGER FAMILY, AND NATIVE TO INDIA, INDONESIA AND CHINA. TODAY IT IS ALSO CULTIVATED IN SOUTH AMERICA AND THE CARIBBEAN. THE ROOT RESEMBLES THE GINGER ROOT, WITH SHORT 'FINGERS' GROWING OUT OF THE UNDERGROUND STEM OF THE PLANT.

Sitting on the roof of a small diesel-engined wooden boat next to the captain, wrapped in a blanket and warming my hands on tea that I had brought along in my thermos flask, I could see the sea and land joining together on the far distant horizon. Our boat passed between queues of palm trees lining the edges of the back waters that flowed between green paddy fields, their beauty revealed by the sunrise. The only sound that disturbed the early morning tranquillity came from the hammering of the boat's engine.

This unique journey had begun in the south of India, in Aleppey. To pass the time there, while I waited to begin my boat trip, I wandered around the village. In a dusty, narrow back-alley, I came across a street market where the traders were setting up for a hopefully busy day.

One of the traders caught my attention. His head was elegantly covered with a brilliant white turban, and his snow-white moustache skilfully curled up at each end. He was surrounded by open sacks whose holes were held together with a few rough stitches. They were full of strangely shaped roots, a few of which were cut lengthwise in half to show bright orange flesh. I took a few in my hand and tried to smell them. Seeing this the old man gestured me closer, and engaged me in a fascinating conversation. His dark eyes twinkling, he tried to convince me that he was selling saffron. But what I saw in the sacks bore no resemblance to the spice that I remembered as saffron from college and that I had tasted in my own country. I recognised that these roots were turmeric – but fresh!

In Malaysia, where it is called manjal, I also came across fresh turmeric, and occasionally I see it in Asian shops in London. But most commonly, the roots are boiled, dried and ground to produce a nutty, slightly bitter, aromatic powder, which can vary in shade from bright yellow to yellowish-brown.

Turmeric is most commonly used as one of the main ingredients in curry powder. In its own right it will add its characteristic golden colour and a wonderful pungent aroma to any dish. I find it particularly good with rice, fish, tomatoes and onions. A pinch in a creamy sauce will add an elusive peppery taste. In the West, it is used commercially to colour sauces and processed foods, and it is often added to blended mustards.

I also learnt from that wise old man that turmeric is the most sacred spice of the Hindu and is an element of both religious and social rituals in some parts of India. It is also used traditionally as a remedy for all sorts of ailments and as a disinfectant, with turmeric water sprinkled to prevent the spread of infectious diseases.

Its usefulness does not end there: for centuries turmeric has been used as a textile dye; in some parts of India it is worked to a paste and applied as a beauty mask; and on many Pacific islands it is believed to have magical properties and to ward off evil spirits!

A WORLD OF FLAVOURS

TURMERIC

Crunchy Vegetable and Goat's Cheese Salad

Serves 4

- 2 tsp sesame seeds
- 1 tsp finely chopped fresh coriander (cilantro)
- 1 tsp finely chopped parsley
- 300 g/1 x 11 oz St. Maurice goat's cheese, or other rindless, cylindrical, firm but not dry goat's cheese, chilled
- 2 tbsp flour
- 1 tsp mild turmeric
- 1 egg, lightly beaten
- 2 tbsp sunflower oil

Dressing

- 3 tbsp sunflower oil
- ½ garlic clove, peeled and crushed with a knife or garlic press
- 2 tsp curry powder
- 50 g/2 oz (½ cup) red sweet pepper, cut into fine strips
- 50 g/2 oz (½ cup) yellow sweet pepper, cut into fine strips
- 1 tbsp white wine
- 50 ml/2 fl oz chicken stock (see basic recipe, page 190)
- ½ lemon, juiced
- 1 tsp light soy sauce
- 1 tsp balsamic vinegar
- salt and freshly ground pepper

Garnish

- 12 leaves white chicory (Belgian endive)
- 50 g/2 oz mixed salad leaves
- 1 spring onion (green onion), cut into fine rings

(Approximately 510 calories per portion)

This salad requires quite a few ingredients and some time for preparation, but the combination of the turmeric-flavoured goat's cheese and the crunchiness of the toasted sesame seeds gives a distinguished flavour worth the effort.

Dressing

Put 2 tbsp of the sunflower oil in a saucepan. Heat, then add the crushed garlic and curry powder and sweat for 20 seconds without colouring. Add the red and yellow peppers and sweat for a further minute without colouring. Add the white wine and bring to the boil. Add the chicken stock, return to the boil and simmer for 2–3 minutes. Then remove from heat and add the lemon juice, soy sauce, balsamic vinegar and remaining sunflower oil. Season and allow to cool.

Cheese

Toast the sesame seeds on a baking tray under the grill (broiler). (Keep your eyes on them as they will burn easily.) As soon as they are golden brown, remove from the grill and cool. When cold, mix them with the finely chopped herbs.

Cut the cheese into 12 slices, each about 1 cm/½ inch thick: this will give 3 slices per person. Place the slices on a tray and sprinkle half the herb mixture on top. Press lightly with your fingers. Gently turn the slices over and sprinkle with the remaining herb mixture. Press lightly again. Keep aside.

To Finish

When ready to serve, arrange 3 leaves of chicory in a star shape on each plate. Remove the peppers from the dressing, keeping the dressing to one side until later, and toss the peppers with the salad leaves and spring onion. Place in the centre of the chicory 'star'. Set the plates to one side.

Mix together the flour and turmeric, and have ready the lightly beaten egg. Gently heat the oil in a non-stick pan.

Now dust both sides of each slice of cheese with the turmeric flour and press on lightly with your hands. Dip each cheese slice into beaten egg and remove, allowing any excess egg to drip off. Place directly into the hot oil and fry gently until golden on both sides, turning the slices gently. Remove to paper towels to drain.

Place the warm cheese slices between the chicory leaves on each plate. Pour a little more dressing over the salad and serve immediately.

Mussel and Salmon Soup

(Approximately 520 calories per portion)

A substantial fish soup that will delight mussel lovers.

Mussels
Scrub each mussel individually under running water, and remove the 'beard' if necessary. Rinse twice more in fresh water to ensure that all the sand is removed. Discard any mussels that are not tightly closed.

Soup
Heat the olive oil in a saucepan large enough to hold all the mussels. Add the chopped shallots and garlic. Cook for about 1 minute without colouring. Add the cleaned mussels and the white wine. Cover with a lid, bring to the boil and simmer gently for 5 minutes. Remove from the heat. Remove the mussels from the saucepan, and pass the cooking liquid through a very fine sieve into a bowl. Put it to one side.

Using only the mussels with open shells, remove all but 8 of them from their shells (keep the 8 mussels in shell for the garnish); put aside. Discard any mussels with shells that have remained firmly shut.

Now melt the butter in a saucepan and sweat the leek, carrot and fennel with the turmeric for about 1 minute without colouring. Add the reserved mussel cooking liquid and the fish stock and bring to the boil. Add the cream and cook for about 5 minutes or until a smooth consistency is obtained. Season with salt, pepper and a pinch of cayenne.

To Finish
Reduce the heat and add the salmon cubes and mussels, including the ones in shells. Stir gently. Simmer for 30 seconds. Add the chopped coriander and serve.

Serves 4

800 g/1 3/4 lb fresh mussels
2 tbsp olive oil
50 g/2 oz (1/3 cup) shallots, peeled and chopped
1/2 garlic clove, peeled and crushed with a knife or garlic press
200 ml/7 fl oz dry white wine
25 g/1 oz (2 tbsp) butter
50 g/2 oz (1/3 cup) white of leek, cut into 3 mm/1/8 inch dice
40 g/1 1/2 oz (1/3 cup) peeled carrot, cut into 3 mm/1/8 inch dice
25 g/1 oz (1/4 cup) bulb fennel, cut into 3 mm/1/8 inch dice
1 tsp turmeric
400 ml/14 fl oz fish stock (see basic recipe, page 190)
300 ml/10 fl oz double cream (heavy cream)
salt and freshly ground pepper
cayenne pepper
75 g/3 oz salmon fillet, cut into 1 cm/1/2 inch cubes
1/2 tsp finely chopped fresh coriander (cilantro)

A WORLD OF FLAVOURS

Mussel and Salmon Soup
(page 37)

TURMERIC

Aubergine Soup

Serves 4

25 g/1 oz (2 tbsp) unsalted butter
1 shallot, peeled and finely chopped
½ garlic clove, peeled and crushed with a knife or garlic press
¼ tsp turmeric
¼ tsp mild curry powder
450 g/1 lb aubergines (eggplants), peeled, and end removed, cut into slices 3 mm/⅛ inch thick
1 medium-sized tomato, peeled, seeded and cut into quarters
750 ml/1 ¼ pt (3 cups) chicken stock (see basic recipe, page 190)
150 ml/5 fl oz single cream (light cream)
¼ tsp grated nutmeg
salt and freshly ground pepper

Garnish

1 tbsp chopped almonds
2 spring onions (green onions), cut into fine rings

Grill (broiler)

On highest setting

(Approximately 160 calories per portion)

Although curry powder already contains a substantial amount of turmeric, this recipe adds yet more to boost the flavour and colour of the aubergine. Before use, the spices are pan-fried to strengthen their flavour – a technique I brought back from my travelling in Sri Lanka.

Soup
Melt the butter in a saucepan and sweat the shallots and garlic until translucent, without colouring. Stir in the turmeric and curry powder and cook for 1 minute. Add the aubergines and tomato and cook for a further 2 minutes, stirring constantly. Add the chicken stock, bring to the boil and simmer for 20 minutes.

Add the cream and simmer for a further 5 minutes. Then add the nutmeg and season. Use a hand blender or food processor to purée the soup, then pass it through a sieve back into a saucepan.

Garnish
Whilst the soup is simmering, toast the almonds under the grill (broiler) until golden brown. Make sure you keep your eye on them as they tend to burn easily. Allow to cool, then wrap in a clean kitchen towel and crush gently with your hands. Keep aside.

To Finish
When ready to eat, bring the soup to the boil. Pour into 4 warmed soup bowls and sprinkle with the toasted almonds and spring onion rings.

Creamed Coconut and Pumpkin Soup

Serves 6

2 tbsp vegetable oil
400 g/¼ oz (2 cups) peeled pumpkin, cut into thumb-sized cubes
1 onion, peeled and sliced
2 garlic cloves, peeled and crushed with a knife or garlic press
1 tsp turmeric
1 tsp mild curry powder
2 tbsp flour
50 g/2 oz (¼ cup) canned unsweetened coconut cream (thick coconut milk)
1 lt/1 ¾ pt (1 qt) vegetable stock (see basic recipe, page 193)
1 tbsp white wine vinegar
salt and freshly ground pepper

Garnish

2 tbsp sunflower seeds, toasted and coarsely chopped
1 tbsp finely chopped fresh chives

Grill (broiler)

On highest setting

(Approximately 140 calories per portion)

This soup has a unique flavour which I've encountered in many dishes in the Far East, where coconut is combined with turmeric.

Heat the vegetable oil in a saucepan. Add the pumpkin, onion and garlic and sweat for 3 minutes or until the onion is translucent but not coloured. Stir in the turmeric and curry powder and sweat for a further minute. Stir in the flour. Add the coconut cream and the cold vegetable stock and bring to the boil. Reduce the heat and simmer for 20 minutes.

Remove from the heat and allow to cool slightly, then purée the mixture in a blender or food processor. Return the soup to the saucepan and bring back to the boil.

To Finish
Add the vinegar and season with salt and freshly ground pepper. Sprinkle over the chopped sunflower seeds and chives and serve.

Fillet of sea bass with Indian spices

(Approximately 360 calories per portion)

In this recipe, 'pockets' of sea bass are filled with a curried vegetable mixture and served in a creamy sauce. To ensure a neat presentation, score the skin of the fish well to prevent it curling up when cooked, and do not overfill the pockets or the stuffing will pop out.

Filling
Wash and trim the fennel. Cut it into quarters and then into very thin slices. Heat the oil in a saucepan, add the fennel and chopped shallot and sweat until translucent, without colouring. Stir in the curry powder and sweat for a further minute on medium heat. Add the cream and bring to the boil. Stirring constantly, boil to reduce until most of the liquid has evaporated and the mixture has the consistency of soft cheese. Add the diced tomato, and season. Remove from the heat and allow to cool, then refrigerate until completely cold.

Fish
Using a sharp knife, cut the fish into 4 equal squarish pieces. Score the skin of each piece (to prevent the fish curling up when cooked). Now what you are going to do is to form a 'pocket' in each piece into which you will put the cold filling. To do this, put one piece in front of you, skin side down. With the sharp knife, cut a slit along the edge of one side, about halfway between the skin and the top surface. Cut gently into the piece of fish, leaving about 5 mm/¼ inch intact along the other 3 sides. Repeat the process with the other 3 pieces of fish.

Season the fish with salt and pepper. Divide the cold filling into four and, using a teaspoon, pack it into each 'pocket'. Heat the oil in a non-stick pan. Place the fish pieces in the pan, skin side down, and brown lightly. Turn over and brown the other side. Remove to a baking tray and bake in the preheated oven for 4-6 minutes or until cooked. Please note that the fish will shrink a little and some of the stuffing will be pushed out. Remove from the oven and leave to rest in a warm place on a rack.

Sauce
Combine the fish stock, white wine, shallot and garlic in a saucepan and bring to the boil. Simmer for 1 minute over a medium heat. Add the curry powder and the cream and boil for 1 minute. Add the tomato strips and season.

To Finish
To serve, divide the sauce among 4 warm plates and place the fish on top. To add a finishing touch, garnish with coriander leaves.

Serves 4

700 g/1 ½ lb sea bass fillet
2 tbsp vegetable oil
fresh coriander leaves (cilantro), to garnish

Filling

40 g/1 ½ oz bulb fennel
1 tbsp vegetable oil
½ shallot, peeled and finely chopped
½ tsp curry powder
4 tbsp double cream (heavy cream)
1 small tomato, peeled, seeded and diced
salt and freshly ground pepper

Sauce

100 ml/4 fl oz fish stock (see basic recipe, page 190)
50 ml/2 fl oz white wine
¼ shallot, peeled and finely chopped
¼ garlic clove, peeled and crushed with a knife or garlic press
1 tbsp curry powder
100 ml/4 fl oz double cream (heavy cream)
3 medium-sized tomatoes, peeled, seeded and cut in half, then cut into 5 mm/¼ inch strips

Oven temperature

170°C/325°F/Gas mark 3

Oven-baked Aubergine and Smoked Mackerel

Serves 4

- 4 small aubergines (eggplants), each about 12 cm/5 inches long
- vegetable oil to brush the aubergine
- salt and freshly ground pepper

Filling

- 2 tbsp vegetable oil
- 1 shallot, peeled and finely chopped
- ½ garlic clove, peeled and crushed with a knife or garlic press
- 1 tsp turmeric
- 1 courgette (zucchini), peeled and cut into small dice
- 1 medium-sized ripe tomato, peeled, seeded and coarsely chopped
- 2 medium-sized smoked mackerel

Sauce

- 1 tbsp vegetable oil
- 1 shallot, peeled and finely chopped
- 1 tsp curry powder
- 100 ml/4 fl oz fish stock (see basic recipe, page 190)
- 100 ml/4 fl oz single cream (light cream)
- 2 tbsp plain yoghurt
- 1 tsp finely chopped fresh coriander leaves (cilantro)

Oven temperature
180°C/350°F/Gas mark 4

(Approximately 357 calories per portion)

Turmeric is used here to add a subtle flavour to the aubergine and smoked mackerel boats, which are served with a yoghurt sauce. No further accompaniment is needed.

Aubergines

Cut the aubergines lengthwise in half. Remove most of the flesh with a teaspoon, leaving 1 cm/½ inch of flesh intact against the skin. Score this flesh with a sharp knife, without piercing the skin. Each half aubergine should now look like a small boat. Brush the inside of each with vegetable oil and season with salt and pepper. Place the aubergine boats, skin side up, on a greased baking tray and bake in the preheated oven for about 15 minutes or until cooked.

Filling

In the meantime, chop the scooped-out aubergine flesh coarsely. Heat the vegetable oil in a non-stick pan, add the chopped aubergine, shallots and garlic, and cook for 2 minutes. Stir in the turmeric and sweat for a further minute without colouring. Add the courgette and tomato, and season. Cover with a lid and reduce the heat. Simmer gently for about 10 minutes.

Remove the skin and bones from the mackerel and flake the meat into small finger-sized pieces.

When the vegetables are cooked, remove from heat. Mix in the flaked mackerel and adjust the seasoning. Spoon the mixture into the aubergine boats and arrange in an ovenproof dish. Keep aside.

Sauce

Heat the vegetable oil in a saucepan and sweat the shallot with the curry powder for 1–2 minutes without colouring. Add the fish stock, bring to the boil and allow to simmer until reduced to half of the volume. Add the cream and simmer for a further 3 minutes. Season with salt and freshly ground pepper. Pass through a sieve into a clean saucepan. Keep aside.

To Finish

About 15 minutes before eating, place the filled aubergine boats in the oven and bake for about 10 minutes or until hot. Whilst they are in the oven, finish the sauce: bring it back to the boil, then remove from heat and add the yoghurt and half the coriander. Adjust the seasoning to taste. Remove the aubergines from the oven, and sprinkle with the remaining coriander. Serve the sauce separately.

Tropical Mango Chicken

(Approximately 245 calories per portion)

As in many recipes, the sauce here needs to be reduced to ensure the right flavour and consistency. The difficulty is always to judge just how much a sauce should be reduced. To help, use the handle of a wooden spoon as a gauge: dip it into the sauce before starting the reduction, to 'measure' the quantity, then use this 'measurement' to judge a half, quarter and so on.

Marinating
Brush each chicken breast with soy sauce and leave in a cool place to marinate for 10-15 minutes.

Mango
Peel the mango. Cut one half into small dice and chop the other half coarsely for the sauce. Keep both aside separately.

Sauce
Heat the butter in a saucepan. Add the shallots, garlic and coarsely chopped mango and sweat until translucent. Stir in the turmeric and sweat for another minute. Add the vinegar and sherry. Bring to the boil and simmer for 1 minute. Add all but 50 ml/2 fl oz of the chicken stock. Bring back to the boil and simmer to reduce to half the original volume. Pass through a fine sieve into a clean saucepan.

Mix the cornflour with the reserved cold chicken stock. Add a little of the hot liquid to it, then whisk it all back into the sauce in the pan. Bring to the boil and season. Keep to one side.

Chicken breasts
Heat the oil in a non-stick pan. Season the chicken breasts with salt and freshly ground pepper and add to the pan. Brown them on both sides. Remove them to a roasting tray. (Keep the non-stick pan to one side, as you will need it again.) Roast the breasts in the preheated oven until cooked but not dry. Remove them from the tray and keep warm.

To Finish
Using the non-stick pan, fry the diced mango for 2-3 seconds.

To serve, arrange the diced mango on a warm dish and place the chicken breasts on top. Heat the sauce and pour it over the chicken and mango. Serve immediately.

Serves 4

4 skinless chicken breasts (breast halves)
1 tsp light soy sauce
1 ripe, sweet mango
2 tbsp vegetable oil
salt and freshly ground pepper

Sauce

50 g/2 oz (4 tbsp) butter
100 g/4 oz (2/3 cup) shallots, peeled and finely chopped
1/2 garlic clove, peeled and finely chopped
1/2 tsp mild turmeric
2 tsp raspberry vinegar
2 tsp dry sherry
600 ml/1 pint (2 1/2 cups) brown chicken stock (see basic recipe, page 191)
2 tsp cornflour (cornstarch)

Oven temperature

170°C/325°F/Gas mark 3

Honey Chicken Thighs

Serves 3

25 g/1 oz (2 tbsp) butter
1 tbsp honey, preferably clear
1 tsp prepared English mustard
½ tsp turmeric
½ tsp curry powder
salt and freshly ground pepper
6 chicken thighs

Sauce

1 tbsp plain yoghurt
2 tbsp single cream (light cream)
1 tsp chopped fresh coriander (cilantro)
½ tsp chopped parsley

Oven temperature

170°C/325°F/Gas mark 3

(Approximately 360 calories per portion)

This is such a simple recipe, but the result is irresistible. The marinade gives the thighs a sticky, slightly spicy coating, which is complemented by the coriander and yoghurt dipping sauce. When baking the chicken, keep an eye on the temperature - the honey in the marinade has a tendency to burn quite easily.

Chicken
Melt the butter in a frying pan. Add the honey, mustard, turmeric, curry powder, salt and pepper and stir until mixed. Remove from the heat. Roll the thighs in the mixture to coat and place them in an ovenproof dish. Bake in the preheated oven for 30-35 minutes or until cooked and tender.

Sauce
Whilst the chicken is cooking, prepare the sauce by simply mixing all the ingredients together.

To Finish
Serve the chicken hot, with the sauce handed separately.

Braised Turmeric Chicken

Serves 4

½ tsp turmeric
½ sachet saffron (about 6 threads)
2 tbsp vegetable oil
100 g/4 oz (²⁄₃ cup) peeled onion, chopped
2 garlic cloves, peeled and crushed with a knife or garlic press
4 chicken breasts (breast halves)
salt and freshly ground pepper
2 tbsp chopped fresh coriander (cilantro)
1 tbsp chopped fresh flat-leaf parsley
2 beef tomatoes, chopped
2 tbsp dry sherry
200 ml/7 fl oz brown chicken stock (see basic recipe, page 191)

Oven temperature

180°C/350°F/Gas mark 4

(Approximately 285 calories per portion)

This is a recipe I've adapted from a dish prepared by my Moroccan chef, Yusri Ahmed Tahir. It embodies a unique flavour combination: turmeric and saffron. If you're tempted to try it once, like me, you're bound to make it again.

Mix together the turmeric and saffron. Heat the vegetable oil in a non-stick pan. Add the onion, garlic and spice mixture. Sweat for 2 minutes without colouring. Season the chicken breasts, add to the pan and brown them on both sides. Remove the chicken and keep to one side.

Add the coriander, parsley and tomatoes to the pan and simmer for 2 minutes. Add the sherry and chicken stock, cover and leave to simmer for 7 minutes.

Using a hand blender or food processor, blend the mixture to a smooth sauce. Season.

To Finish
Put the chicken into an ovenproof dish and pour over the sauce. Simmer gently, covered, in the preheated oven for 10 minutes. This is a rustic dish and should be served in the cooking dish.

Steak with Sweet Potato Sauce

(Approximately 420 calories per portion)

I discovered sweet potatoes in Indonesia, where they are most often eaten as a vegetable, fried or cut into chunks and cooked in sweetened coconut milk and sugar. Sometimes they are used in sauces, which was the inspiration for this recipe. The sauce goes well with any cut of beef, particularly if it is barbecued. The turmeric gives a bold colour and a slightly peppery taste, whilst the sweetness is counterbalanced by a squeeze of lemon.

Sauce

Heat the vegetable oil in a non-stick pan. Add the chopped shallot and garlic and sweat until translucent, without colouring. Stir in the ginger and turmeric and sweat for another minute. Add the sweet potato, vegetable stock and desiccated coconut. Bring to the boil and simmer for about 10 minutes or until the sweet potato is cooked.

Using a hand blender or food processor, purée the sauce, then pass through a sieve into a clean saucepan. Bring to the boil, add the lemon juice and season to taste. Keep aside.

To Finish

Season the steak on both sides with salt and pepper, then brush with oil. Grill or pan-fry over medium heat for 5–7 minutes or until cooked to your taste. Heat the sauce and serve with the steak.

Serves 2

1 tbsp vegetable oil
2 rump steaks (boneless sirloin steaks), each 150 g/5 oz

Sauce

2 tbsp vegetable oil
½ shallot, peeled and finely chopped
¼ garlic clove, peeled and crushed with a knife or garlic press
1 pinch of ginger, finely chopped fresh or ground
1 tsp turmeric
100 g/4 oz (½ cup) peeled sweet potato, diced
300 ml/10 fl oz vegetable stock (see basic recipe, page 193)
1 tsp desiccated coconut (dried unsweetened shredded coconut)
squeeze of lemon
salt and freshly ground pepper

Medallions of Lamb with a Turmeric Crust

(Approximately 550 calories per portion)

This is an extremely tasty dish. The crust can be used not only with lamb but also with other meats and poultry, too. It can be made well in advance and even frozen if so desired.

Turmeric crust

Beat the butter until it turns 'white'. Add the garlic, mustard, egg yolk and turmeric and mix thoroughly. Gently fold in the herbs and brioche crumbs. Add the lemon juice, Worcestershire sauce and seasoning and mix thoroughly. Taste and adjust the seasoning if necessary. Shape into a 'sausage' about 15 cm/6 inches long, with a diameter to match the size of the lamb medallions, and wrap in greaseproof paper (wax paper). Keep in the refrigerator until required.

Meat

Heat the vegetable oil in a pan. Season the medallions of lamb with salt and freshly ground pepper, then brown the meat on both sides in the hot oil. Remove to a baking tray and roast in the preheated oven for about 5 minutes. Remove from the oven and take off the tray. Leave to rest for 3–4 minutes.

To Finish

Place the medallions of lamb on a baking tray, leaving at least 2.5 cm/1 inch space between each piece of meat. Slice the turmeric butter into 5 mm/¼ inch slices and place one on top of each medallion. Place under the preheated grill (broiler) until the crust is golden brown. Carefully remove from the baking tray to a serving dish. Garnish with herbs and serve.

Serves 6

2 tbsp vegetable oil
900 g/2 lb loin of lamb, cut into 12 equal pieces (2 per person)
salt and freshly ground pepper
fresh thyme and rosemary, to garnish

Turmeric crust

125 g/4 oz (½ cup) butter, at room temperature
½ clove garlic, peeled and crushed with a knife or garlic press
¼ tsp French whole-grain mustard
1 egg yolk
¼ tsp turmeric
1 tsp finely chopped parsley
½ tsp finely chopped fresh coriander (cilantro)
½ tsp finely chopped fresh chervil
50 g/2 oz (1 cup) brioche crumbs
¼ lemon, juiced
Worcestershire sauce to taste

Oven temperature

170°C/325°F/Gas mark 3

Grill (broiler)

very hot

A WORLD OF FLAVOURS

*Medallions of
Lamb with a
Turmeric Crust
(page 45)*

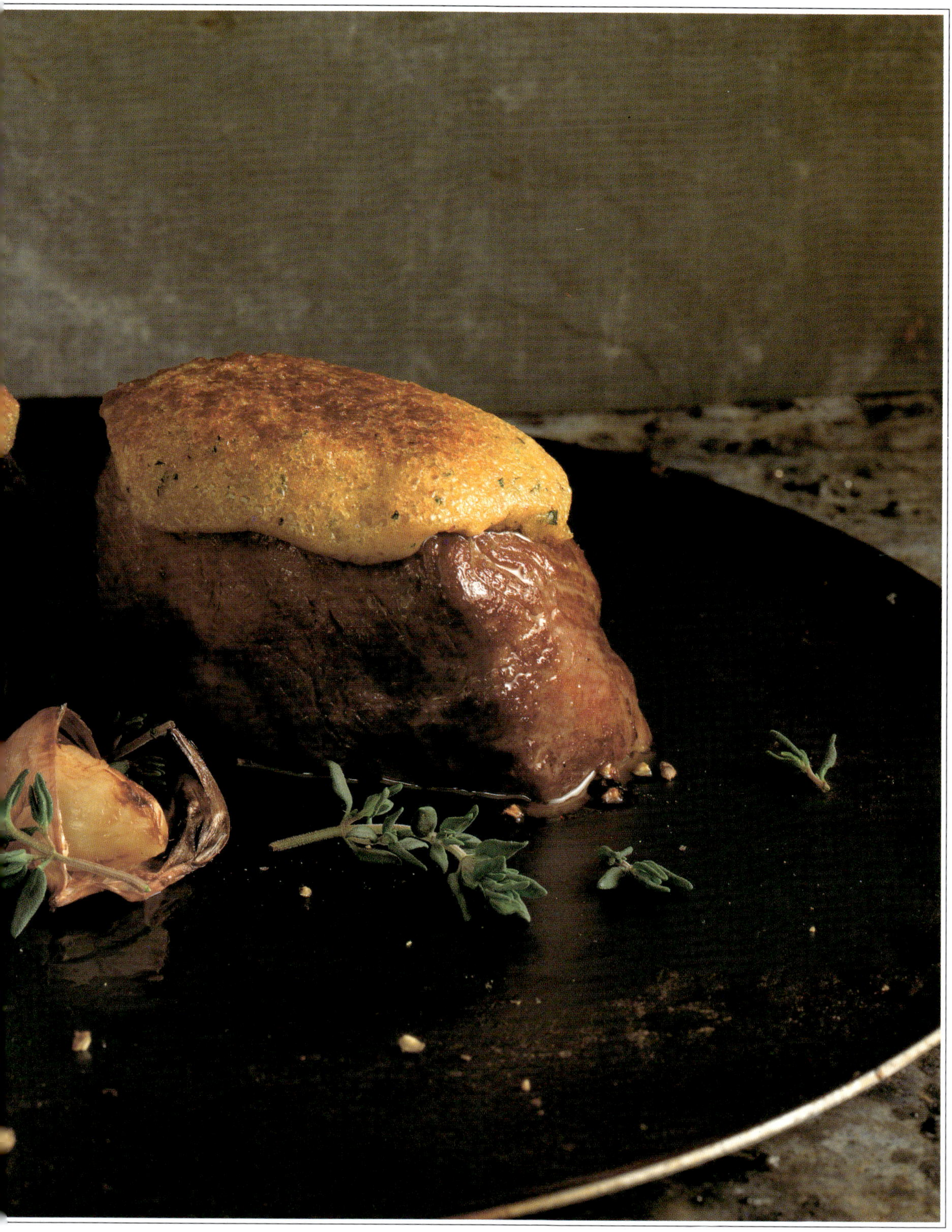

Peppers Filled with Minced Lamb

Serves 4

- 4 medium-sized red sweet peppers
- 1 slice of white bread
- 175 ml/6 fl oz milk
- 2 tbsp vegetable oil
- 1 shallot, peeled and finely chopped
- 1 garlic clove, peeled and crushed with a knife or garlic press
- 4 bay leaves
- 1 tsp turmeric
- 1 tbsp white wine vinegar
- 2 tsp sugar
- 1 tbsp raisins
- 250 g/9 oz minced lamb
- salt and freshly ground pepper
- 1 egg
- fresh basil leaves, to garnish

Oven temperature
170°C/325°F/ Gas mark 3

(Approximately 360 calories per portion)

This is based on a South African dish which was first made for me by my mother-in-law at Plettenberg Bay. I've adapted her recipe, and use the spicy, slightly sweet lamb mixture to fill the halves of a red pepper, which are then baked in the oven. Serve this with Mandoub's rice (see page 189).

Peppers

Cut the peppers in half lengthwise and remove the seeds with a small knife. Bring a large pot of water to the boil and plunge the peppers into it. Boil for 1 minute, then remove from the heat and take out the peppers using a slotted spoon. Immediately refresh them in a bowl of iced water. When cold, drain and pat dry with paper towel. Keep aside.

Filling

Soak the bread in the milk until it is soft, then squeeze out any excess milk. Keep the bread aside; reserve the milk.

Heat the vegetable oil in a frying pan. Add the shallots and garlic and sweat until golden brown in colour. Add the bay leaves, turmeric, vinegar, sugar and raisins, followed by the minced meat. Allow to cook gently for 2 minutes. Add the soaked bread to the mixture and season with salt and freshly ground pepper. Remove from the heat, and discard the bay leaves.

To Finish

Divide the meat filling into 8 equal portions and carefully fill the blanched pepper halves. Place the filled peppers on a roasting tray.

Mix the reserved milk with the beaten egg and season lightly with salt and freshly ground pepper. Carefully pour over the filling in the peppers; do not allow the mixture to overflow. Bake in the preheated oven for 40 minutes.

Garnish with basil and serve immediately.

Pumpkin and Cashew Nut Cake

(Approximately 475 calories per slice)

This simple cake contains two ingredients more usually found in savoury dishes: pumpkin and turmeric. However, used in this way they result in a cake that is quite outstanding. It is moist and dense in texture, and sandwiched together with a rich cheese filling.

Cake

Grease the cake pan and line the bottom with greaseproof paper (wax paper).

Sift the flour, turmeric, bicarbonate of soda, baking powder, cinnamon and salt into a large bowl. Add the caster sugar. Make a well in the centre and add the lightly beaten eggs, the oil and vanilla. Stir to combine the ingredients thoroughly. Fold in the pumpkin, cashew nuts, apple, orange peel and sultanas, mixing well.

Spoon the mixture into the prepared cake pan. Place in the centre of the preheated oven and bake for about 1 hour 20 minutes or until a skewer inserted into the centre of the cake comes out clean.

When the cake is cooked, remove it from the oven and let it cool in the pan, on a rack, for 15 minutes. Then turn it out on to the rack and remove the paper. Allow the cake to cool completely.

Filling

In a bowl, cream the butter until light. Add the cheese and mix well to combine. (Don't over-beat once the creamy cheese has been added or the mixture will separate.) Sift the icing sugar, a little at a time, into the bowl and mix well. Chill before use.

To Finish

When the cake is completely cold, cut it in half horizontally. Spread the filling evenly on the bottom layer, using a palette knife (metal spatula). Place the other layer on top. Gently set a plate (about 2.5 cm/1 inch smaller than the cake) upside down on top of the cake. Sift icing sugar around the border, then carefully remove the plate.

MAKES 1 CAKE / 12 PORTIONS

200 g/7 oz plain flour
(1 ⅓ cups all-purpose flour)

¼ tsp turmeric

1 tsp bicarbonate of soda (baking soda)

1 tsp baking powder

1 tsp ground cinnamon

¼ tsp salt

175 g/6 oz caster sugar
(¾ cup granulated sugar)

3 eggs, lightly beaten

120 ml/4 ½ fl oz vegetable oil

½ tsp vanilla essence (vanilla extract)

150 g/ 5 oz (1 ⅓ cups)
grated raw pumpkin

50 g/2 oz (½ cup) cashew nuts, chopped

75 g/3 oz (¾ cup) grated apple,
(preferably Golden Delicious)

50 g/2 oz (⅓ cup) candied orange peel,
coarsely chopped

50 g/2 oz sultanas
(⅓ cup golden raisins)

icing sugar (confectioners' sugar),
to finish

Filling

125 g/5 oz (10 tbsp) butter

100 g/4 oz (½ cup) soft creamy cheese

225 g/9 oz icing sugar
(2 cups confectioners' sugar)

You will need

a round loose-bottomed
cake pan, 23 cm/9 inches in diameter

Oven temperature

170°C/325°F/Gas mark 3

Apricot Crumble

Serves 4

19 large, ripe apricots, cut in half and stone removed

Sauce

100 g/4 oz caster sugar
(½ cup granulated sugar)

1 pinch of ground cinnamon

1 vanilla pod split (vanilla bean), lengthwise in half

½ lemon, juiced

200 ml/7 fl oz orange juice

3 tbsp quark (soft creamy cheese), or you can use fromage frais or cream cheese

Crumble

150 g/5 oz plain flour
(1 cup all-purpose flour)

½ tsp turmeric

75 g/3 oz (6 tsp) butter, at room temperature

50 g/2 oz (½ cup) peeled almonds, finely chopped

80 g/3 ½ oz demerara sugar
(6 ½ tbsp raw brown sugar)

Garnish

icing sugar (confectioners' sugar)
fresh mint

Oven temperature

200°C/400°F/Gas mark 6

Grill (broiler)

very hot

(Approximately 650 calories per portion)

Tangy apricots, topped with a nutty crumble and served with a creamy apricot sauce. Delicious!

Sauce

Put the caster sugar, cinnamon and vanilla pod into a medium-sized saucepan. Add the lemon and orange juices and bring to the boil. Add the apricot halves and return to the boil. Cover with a lid and simmer very gently for 1 minute. Allow to cool.

Drain the syrup completely from the fruit. Keep the fruit aside. Bring the syrup back to the boil and add 6 of the apricot halves to it. Simmer until the apricots are soft, then remove the vanilla pod.

Purée the mixture in a blender to the consistency of a sauce. Pass through a sieve into a bowl and whisk in the quark. Keep the sauce aside. Place the remaining apricot halves in an ovenproof dish and keep aside.

Crumble mix

Mix the flour with the turmeric. Rub in the butter with your finger-tips until the mixture resembles fine breadcrumbs. Add the almonds and sugar.

To Finish

Sprinkle the crumble over the apricots and bake in the preheated oven for about 5 minutes. Then brown under the preheated grill (broiler). Dust with icing sugar, garnish with mint and serve hot, with the sauce at room temperature.

Chillies

Chilli peppers are, in fact, the seed pods of plants belonging to the capsicum family. They vary in colour from green to red, orange or yellow when fresh (reddish-black or brown when dried), and in size from 5 mm (1/4 inch) to 30 cm (12 inch) giants. They vary in pungency, too, with the larger ones being quite mild – generally, the smaller the chilli the hotter it will be. The small birdseye and habenero chillies are the real devils!

I have unforgettable memories for the many 'tears' I have shed over dishes containing chilli peppers, or hot peppers, but perhaps the most memorable of all was in Sri Lanka. For many months I travelled around that beautiful island where chillies play an important role in the cooking, most particularly in curry dishes.

My travelling companion and I discovered that hotly spiced food is an acquired taste, but once acquired it is quite possible to get hooked on it! At first, when we went for a bite to eat, if asked if we liked our food 'mild', 'medium spiced' or 'hot' we opted for mild, just to be sure. But, like most Westerners, after a couple of weeks, we felt sure that we were more accustomed to the food and that our tastebuds were 'tuned in'.

So at our next meal, at a small family guest house, we decided to be more adventurous. Seated at a table on wobbly chairs, beneath a colonial fan cooling the air, we gave our order to the waiter, who was probably the son of the family: an assortment of curry dishes – hot! He repeated our order, and walked away, only to return to ask if we had said 'hot'. We confidently assured him that we had.

After a while, the dishes appeared, served from an old and bent but highly polished and ornately decorated brass tray. They were placed in front of us and we were told to enjoy our meal.

We started eating. Looking over the shoulder of my friend, I could see what I assumed was the whole family peering around the screen that partially separated the room. They were giggling, and obviously interested to see how we reacted to the food. The young waiter reappeared and asked if everything was okay. I had just swallowed the second bite, and a burning sensation was starting in my throat, but it was cooled down by the air I breathed in to reply to his question. I assured him that everything was excellent. Soon, however, we were perspiring, our noses were running and our eyes were tearing. We tried in vain to cool ourselves down with rice and hot tea. It only became worse.

This experience instilled in me a lingering respect for chillies, and made me realise that they should be used judiciously. In moderation, they will deliciously sharpen the flavour of a dish, but added liberally they can cause strong reactions. When using chillies, always take into account your own palate and those of your friends, and remember that even a small quantity of chilli pepper can burn. To soothe a fiery mouth, eat bread, rice or beans - drinking will only make the burning worse, as I discovered in that guest house in Sri Lanka.

The hottest part of a chilli pepper is centred in the seeds and surrounding membrane, so for flavour without fire, remove these before cooking. Be careful not to touch your eyes or other sensitive areas such as your lips when preparing chillies, and also avoid any cuts - they will burn painfully. Wash your hands and utensils well with hot soapy water when you've finished.

Incidentally, fresh chillies can be kept in the refrigerator for up to 3 weeks, and they freeze well.

Chillies can also be bought dried - whole, crushed or ground into powder. Small whole dried chillies can be used to season oils and vinegars, and both whole and crushed are excellent as a seasoning in sauces and other dishes. There are numerous varieties of chilli powder, each with its own distinct aroma, flavour and pungency ranging from medium to very hot. Handle chilli powder with caution, and don't sniff it - from experience I can tell you that it will leave a burning sensation for hours!

A WORLD OF FLAVOURS

*C*HILLIES

Oriental cucumber and salmon salad

Serves 4

- 1/2 medium-sized cucumber (English hothouse cucumber)
- 2 medium-sized shallots, peeled and finely chopped
- 1 medium-sized tomato, peeled, seeded and cut into small cubes
- 1 tsp chopped fresh dill
- 100 ml/4 fl oz water
- 100 ml/4 fl oz dry white wine
- ¼ bay leaf
- 4 black peppercorns, crushed
- ¼ tsp salt
- 300 g/11 oz salmon fillet, skinned

Dressing
- 50 ml/2 fl oz white wine vinegar
- 40 g/1 ½ oz (3 tbsp) white sugar
- 1 tsp sesame oil
- ¼ tsp salt
- freshly ground pepper
- ¼ tsp finely chopped fresh hot chilli pepper (seeded)

(Approximately 220 calories per portion)

Don't waste the cooking liquid. Pass it through wet muslin and freeze. Use in any recipe requiring fish stock.

Dressing
Mix the vinegar, sugar, sesame oil, salt, pepper and chilli pepper together in a saucepan. Heat gently until the sugar has dissolved, then remove from heat and allow to cool.

Cucumber salad
Cut the cucumber lengthwise in half. Using a teaspoon, remove the seeds. Then cut across into 3 mm/⅛ inch slices and place in a bowl. Add the chopped shallots, tomatoes and dill. Pour over the cold dressing and gently toss together. Marinate for 15 minutes.

Salmon
About 10 minutes before eating, cook the salmon. Mix the water and white wine together in a wide saucepan or sauté pan and bring to the boil. Add the bay leaf, crushed peppercorns and salt. When the mixture is simmering, gently place the salmon fillet in the pan. Simmer for about 1 minute, then turn the fillet over and cook for another minute. Remove the pan from heat and leave the salmon in the warm stock for a further 5 minutes.

To Finish
Remove the salmon from the stock, flake and arrange on a plate. Sprinkle the cucumber and tomato salad on top of the warm salmon and serve immediately.

Spicy mushroom and chicken soup

Serves 4

- 1 tbsp vegetable oil
- 1 skinless boneless chicken breast (breast half), cut into small dice
- salt and freshly ground pepper
- chopped fresh coriander (cilantro), to garnish

Soup
- 2 tbsp vegetable oil
- 1 shallot, peeled and finely chopped
- ½ garlic clove, peeled and crushed with a knife or garlic press
- ¼ tsp finely chopped fresh hot chilli pepper (seeded)
- 1 piece of lemon grass, 2.5 cm/1 inch long
- ½ tsp paprika
- 1 tsp white wine vinegar
- 150 g/5 oz button mushrooms, cut into quarters
- 600 ml/1 pint (2 ½ cups) chicken stock (see basic recipe, page 190)
- 100 ml/4 fl oz single cream (light cream)

(Approximately 170 calories per portion)

A simple soup, full of flavour, with a hint of vinegar to reduce the sweetness.

Chicken
Heat the vegetable oil in a non-stick pan. Season the diced chicken and brown it quickly. Remove from the pan, drain on paper towel and keep aside.

Soup
Heat the vegetable oil in a saucepan. Add the shallot, garlic and chilli pepper and sweat until translucent, without colouring. Add the lemon grass and sprinkle in the paprika. Add the vinegar, mushrooms and chicken stock and bring to the boil. Simmer for 5 minutes. Add the cream and simmer for a further 5 minutes. Season with salt and pepper. Remove from the heat and allow to cool slightly, then discard the lemon grass. Using a hand blender or food processor, purée and then pass through a sieve back into the saucepan.

To Finish
Return the soup to simmering point. Add the diced chicken and leave to rest, off the heat, for 1 minute. Serve sprinkled with chopped coriander.

Piquant Pasta

(Approximately 470 calories per portion)

A quick and easy recipe to delight any pasta lover. The conchiglie can be replaced by another pasta shape as desired. Always cook pasta in ten times as much water, with a spoonful of oil – this will ensure that the pasta does not stick together.

Sauce
Heat the vegetable oil in a saucepan and add the bacon strips, onion, garlic and chilli pepper. Sweat until the onion is translucent, without colouring. Add the tomatoes and vegetable stock. Cover the pan with a lid and simmer for about 1 minute over medium heat. Add the coriander and season with salt and freshly ground pepper. Keep aside.

Pasta
Bring a large pan of salted water to the boil. Add the teaspoon of oil and cook the pasta until 'al dente' (approximately 5 minutes). Drain.

To Finish
Divide the pasta equally between 2 plates. Reheat the sauce and pour it over. Sprinkle with Parmesan cheese, garnish with fresh basil and serve.

Serves 2

200 g/7 oz fresh conchiglie (pasta shells)
1 tsp vegetable oil

Sauce

1 tbsp vegetable oil
2 unsmoked streaky bacon rashers (thick bacon slices), cut across into fine strips
½ onion, peeled and finely chopped
1 garlic clove, peeled and finely chopped
½ tsp finely chopped fresh hot chilli pepper (seeded)
4 medium-sized tomatoes, peeled and coarsely chopped
50 ml/2 fl oz vegetable stock (see basic recipe, page 193)
1 tsp chopped fresh coriander (cilantro)
salt and freshly ground pepper
1 tbsp freshly grated Parmesan cheese
2 sprigs fresh basil, to garnish

Prawn and Sweetcorn Chilli

(Approximately 220 calories per portion)

I have adapted this recipe from the Mexican chilli con carne that our friend, Mariana Gonzales, always hankered after when she felt homesick. Here I have replaced the meat with fresh king prawns, which gives quite a different flavour. I hope Mariana will approve of this.

Beans and Sweetcorn
Cover the red kidney beans with cold water and leave to soak overnight. The next day, drain and cover with fresh salted water. Bring to the boil and boil for 10 minutes, then reduce the heat and cook until tender. Refresh in iced water and drain. Keep aside.

Cook the sweetcorn in boiling salted water for 5 minutes. Immediately refresh in iced water and drain. Using a sharp knife, cut the kernels from the cob and keep aside.

Sauce
Heat the oil in a large saucepan and sweat the shallots and garlic until translucent, without colouring. Add the chilli pepper, spring onions, courgette and sweet peppers and sweat for a further 4 minutes. Add the tomatoes and vegetable stock. Cover the pan and bring to the boil, then simmer for 7 minutes. Add the sweetcorn kernels and red kidney beans.

To Finish
When ready to eat, bring the chilli back to the boil. Add the prawns and simmer gently for 3 minutes. Mix in the sour cream. Taste and season. Sprinkle the chopped basil on top and serve.

Serves 4

100 g/4 oz (⅔ cup) dried red kidney beans
1 ear of fresh sweetcorn
400 g/14 oz fresh raw king prawns (large shrimp), peeled, heads removed

Sauce

1 tbsp olive oil
2 shallots, peeled and finely chopped
1 garlic clove, peeled and crushed with a knife or garlic press
2 tsp finely chopped fresh hot chilli pepper (seeded)
2 spring onions (green onions), finely sliced
1 courgette (zucchini), cut into cubes approximately the same size as the beans
1 red sweet pepper, seeds removed, diced approximately the same size as the beans
1 green sweet pepper, seeds removed, diced approximately the same size as the beans
4 plum tomatoes, peeled and coarsely chopped
100 ml/4 fl oz vegetable stock (see basic recipe, page 193)
1 tbsp sour cream
salt and freshly ground pepper
1 tsp chopped fresh basil

Piquant pasta
(page 57)

Chillies

Three-Pepper Mousse

Makes 4 glasses

250 g/9 oz green sweet peppers
125 g/4 oz red sweet peppers
125 g/4 oz yellow sweet peppers
¼ tsp finely chopped fresh hot chilli pepper (seeded)
50 g/2 oz (⅓ cup) shallots, peeled and finely chopped
100 ml/4 fl oz white wine
100 ml/4 fl oz water
75 ml/3 fl oz olive oil
1 sachet (11.7 g) (1 ½ tbsp) unflavoured gelatine powder
25 g/1 oz (2 tbsp) cooked chopped spinach (stalks removed)
salt and freshly ground pepper
1 tsp tomato paste
500 ml/16 fl oz double cream (heavy cream)
bottled sweet and sour sauce, to serve

Garnish

25 g/1 oz (2 tbsp) butter
12 raw king or tiger prawns (large shrimp), peeled, heads removed
4 leaves of white chicory (Belgian endive)
8 stalks of fresh chives

(Approximately 690 calories per portion)

This dish takes time to prepare, but the result is eye-catching and impressive, served in cocktail glasses.

Mousses

Halve the sweet peppers, remove the seeds and cut each half into chunks. Keep the three peppers separate, according to their colour. To each, add one-third of the chopped chilli pepper. Divide the shallots into thirds. Mix the wine and water and divide among three separate bowls.

Heat one-third of the olive oil in a non-stick pan. Add one portion of shallots and the green peppers and sweat over a low heat for about 2 minutes without colouring. Add one-third of the wine and water mixture. Gently bring to simmering point, then cover the pan with a lid and cook over a low heat for about 10 minutes or until the peppers are tender. Remove the lid and simmer over a low heat for a further 2 minutes. There should still be some liquid remaining in the pan. Remove from the heat and sprinkle over half the gelatine powder (5.5 g). Stir with a metal spoon until completely dissolved. Add the spinach. Purée in a food processor, then press through a medium-sized sieve using a wooden spoon. Season to taste and keep to one side, over a bowl of warm water.

Now repeat the process to make the red pepper mousse, using the red peppers and adding half of the remaining gelatine powder (2.7 g). Add the tomato paste to the mixture before you purée it. Keep warm.

Finally, repeat the same process to make the yellow pepper mousse, using the remaining gelatine. Again, keep the mixture warm.

Whip the cream to a soft ribbon stage. Divide into three portions.

Have ready 4 clean, wide cocktail glasses. Fold one portion of the cream into the green pepper mousse, and divide the mousse among the glasses. Allow to set in the refrigerator for 5 minutes. Mix one portion of the cream into the red pepper mousse and pour over the green pepper mousse. Refrigerate for 5 minutes. Repeat with the yellow pepper mousse, and pour over the red pepper mousse, making three layers in each glass. Cover with plastic film and allow to set in the refrigerator (preferably overnight).

Prawns

Heat the butter in the small pan and add the prawns. Season with salt and freshly ground pepper and cook over moderate heat until pink and opaque. Remove from the pan to paper towels. Allow to cool and keep aside.

To Finish

Remove the film from each glass. Place a chicory leaf and 2 chives vertically in the centre of each mousse. Arrange 3 prawns decoratively around this. Serve immediately, with sweet and sour sauce as an accompaniment.

ℱILLET OF SEA BREAM WITH SHIITAKE MUSHROOMS

(Approximately 600 calories per portion)

I first came across shiitake mushrooms in Chinese cooking where they are used most often in their dried form. Here, however, it's important to use them fresh, because in the dried state they would overpower the subtle flavour of the sea bream.

FISH
Heat 2 tbsp of the oil in a non-stick pan. Season the fillets with salt and freshly ground pepper, then pan-fry very quickly on both sides, skin side first. Remove the fish with a spatula and keep aside.

MUSHROOMS
Using the same pan over a low heat, sweat the shallot and chilli without colouring. Remove them and keep aside on a small plate. Heat the remaining oil in the pan, add the shiitake mushrooms and sweat for about 1 minute, then season with salt and freshly ground pepper. Return the shallot and chilli to the pan and mix thoroughly together.

TO FINISH
Pour the mushroom mixture into an ovenproof dish. Sprinkle over the spring onions and chives, then place the fish fillets on top. Cover with a lid and cook in the preheated oven for about 10 minutes or until the fish is cooked. Garnish the fish with herbs and serve hot.

Serves 2

3 tbsp vegetable oil
4 sea bream fillets (porgy), scales removed
salt and freshly ground pepper
1 shallot, peeled and finely chopped
½ small fresh hot chilli pepper, seeds removed, finely sliced
175 g/6 oz fresh shiitake mushrooms, cut into quarters
2 spring onions (green onions), finely sliced
1 tsp finely chopped fresh chives
fresh chervil and dill, to garnish

Oven temperature
200°C/400°F/Gas mark 6

𝒮IRLOIN STEAK WITH A BLACK OLIVE SAUCE

(Approximately 500 calories per person)

Black olives, chilli and mustard – what a strange combination! But you'll be pleasantly surprised how well they blend together with a tender piece of steak.

STEAK
Heat the oil in a non-stick pan. Season the steaks with salt and pepper and brown them on both sides. Reduce the heat and cook to your required degree. (For medium this will be 7–10 minutes; for rare just under 5 minutes.) Remove from the pan and keep warm in a serving dish.

SAUCE
Using the same pan, heat the oil for the sauce. Add the shallot and sweat until translucent, without colouring. Add the chopped olives and chilli pepper and sweat for a further minute. Add the white wine and stock and bring to the boil. Simmer gently to reduce to half the quantity. Add the cream and simmer until the sauce has a creamy consistency. Remove from the heat and whisk in the mustard. Season, and add the parsley and chives.

TO FINISH
Pour the sauce over the steaks and serve hot.

Serves 4

1 tbsp vegetable oil
4 boneless sirloin steaks
salt and freshly ground white pepper

Sauce

1 tbsp vegetable oil
1 shallot, peeled and finely chopped
6 black olives, finely chopped
¼ tsp finely chopped fresh hot chilli pepper (seeded)
50 ml/2 fl oz white wine
100 ml/4 fl oz brown veal stock (see basic recipe, page 191)
250 ml/8 fl oz single cream (light cream)
1 tbsp whole-grain mustard
2 tsp finely chopped parsley
1 tbsp finely chopped fresh chives

Sirloin Steak with a Black Olive sauce (page 61)

CHILLIES

Roast Marinated Guinea Fowl

Serves 4

4 guinea fowl breasts (breast halves)
1 tbsp vegetable oil
200 g/7 oz fine egg noodles
2 tbsp walnut oil
1 spring onion (green onion), cut into fine rings
¼ tsp finely chopped fresh hot chilli pepper (seeded)
1 shallot, peeled and finely chopped

Marinade

1 tbsp vegetable oil
1 tsp dry sherry
2 tbsp oyster sauce
1 garlic clove, peeled and crushed in a garlic press
salt and freshly ground white pepper

Oven temperature
170°C/325°F/Gas mark 3

(Approximately 425 calories per portion)

Egg noodles form an integral part of Chinese cooking. Here I have given guinea fowl breasts the oriental touch with a marinade that is then used to dress the noodles.

Marinade
Mix the vegetable oil, sherry, oyster sauce and garlic together. Season with salt and freshly ground white pepper. Keep 2 tbsp of this marinade aside for the noodles and brush the guinea fowl breasts with the remainder. Marinate for at least 1–2 hours in the refrigerator.

Guinea Fowl
Heat the oil in a non-stick pan and brown the breasts on both sides. Remove them from the pan and place on a baking tray. Roast in the preheated oven for 10–12 minutes or until cooked but still moist. Remove from the oven and keep warm.

Noodles
Add the noodles to a large pan of boiling salted water and cooked until 'al dente'. Drain. Whilst the noodles are cooking, mix the marinade which was kept to one side with the walnut oil. Add the spring onion rings, chopped chilli pepper and shallot. Adjust the seasoning if necessary.

To Finish
When the noodles are cooked, toss them in the marinade mixture. Place the noodles on a serving dish and arrange the guinea fowl breasts on top. Serve immediately.

Old-Fashioned Pork Stroganoff

Serves 4

2 tbsp vegetable oil
600 g/1 lb 6 oz boneless leg of pork, cut into thumb-sized pieces
salt and freshly ground pepper
2 shallots, peeled and finely sliced
¼ tsp finely chopped fresh hot chilli pepper (seeded)
2 garlic cloves, peeled and crushed with a knife or garlic press
1 tsp mild paprika
2 tbsp flour
100 ml/4 fl oz red wine
300 ml/10 fl oz chicken stock (see basic recipe, page 190)
100 g/4 oz button mushrooms, sliced
1 small red sweet pepper, seeds removed, cut into fine strips
4 tbsp sour cream
4 gherkins, cut into fine strips
¼ tsp English mustard powder, dissolved in 1 tbsp cold water
1 tbsp chopped parsley

Oven temperature
170°C/325°F/Gas mark 3

(Approximately 375 calories per portion)

This old fashioned dish is ideal with either noodles or rice.

Pork
Heat the vegetable oil in a non-stick pan. Season the cubes of pork with salt and freshly ground pepper and add about a quarter of them to the pan. Brown the cubes on all sides, then remove with a slotted spoon and place in an ovenproof dish. Repeat until all the pork is browned.

Sauce
Using the same saucepan and the oil remaining in it, sweat the shallots, chilli pepper and garlic until the shallots are translucent but not coloured. Stir in the paprika and flour. Add the red wine and stock. Bring quickly to the boil, then pour this sauce over the meat. Cover with a lid and allow to simmer in the preheated oven for about 1 hour or until the meat is cooked.

Remove from the oven and add the mushrooms and red pepper. Return to the oven for 5 minutes to cook the pepper.

To Finish
Remove from the oven and stir in the sour cream, gherkins and mustard. Adjust the seasoning and sprinkle with parsley. Serve hot.

Soy Sauce

There are two main types of soy sauce: light and dark. Light soy sauce, which the Chinese often refer to as superior soy, is thinner and saltier than dark. Dark soy sauce owes its almost black colour to a longer ageing process, which also makes it slightly thicker and more strongly flavoured than light soy sauce. When using soy sauce, don't add any salt until the dish is finished. Then taste and decide if additional salt is needed.

A WORLD OF FLAVOURS

SOY SAUCE

My period of study in Osaka, Japan, was one of the most tremendous experiences of my life. I was introduced to a completely different culture, and discovered a new world of traditions and attitudes, not to mention food and cooking.

During my stay, I tried many things and was faced with many new challenges, the first of which was the Japanese language. I spoke only a few words of Japanese when I arrived, and they were very basic. I remember one evening, when I was on my own, trying to order a glass of wine to accompany my dinner. Ordering the food was easy – I pointed to the lovely picture and the young waiter understood immediately what I wanted. But ordering the wine was much more difficult. I was able to communicate the idea of wine, but didn't know how to convey that I wanted only a glass. The waiter called his superior along and again I tried to explain, gesturing with my hands. But we made no headway. Suddenly I had an idea. I took a pencil from my jacket and drew a bottle on a piece of paper with a wine glass next to it. Then I crossed out the bottle and ticked the glass. The head waiter nodded, and my glass was filled with red wine. Success!

Later at the school, I and the other students learnt how to cut a large white radish into paper-thin long strips by using a large knife as sharp as a razor blade. An even greater challenge was learning to write menus in Japanese, using a traditional writing brush. With the help and encouragement of a smiling Japanese girl named Miko, I set to work. The supremely patient master walked up and down the classroom, checking the students' attempts. He stopped at my desk, looked down at my work through his small glasses, then nodded his head and asked me to write the word again. After a while he came back and showed me how easy it is to write with the traditional brush if it is used in the correct way (and if one has had years of practice). He asked me to write the word again, and again and again, and after two hours of practising he approved my work. I was absolutely delighted that the master had approved my writing of the word 'tempura', which is a classic Japanese dish of deep-fried morsels of fish and vegetables in a lacy golden batter.

Another day, I visited a farm where they raise Kobe cattle, which are massaged daily with sake. It is claimed that this treatment produces the finest beef in the world. I also had the opportunity to watch a licensed master prepare the deadly poisonous 'fugu' fish – considered to be a supreme, albeit potentially fatal, delicacy – and then sat at the sashimi bar and chose my meal from a range of raw fish and fish roe. Believe me, I have tried some unusual things in my life, but never raw fish roe. However, not wishing to insult my host, I quickly dipped the roe in soy sauce and ate my first bite – discovering a new range of delicious tastes and sensational textures.

This visit made me realise that I will be a student for the rest of my life, and I returned to England motivated with new ideas and fresh knowledge.

Although I have long known and used soy sauce, one of the things I learned in Japan is how essential soy sauce is in the cooking there. This dark salt liquid is used universally, both as an ingredient and as a table sauce. It is made from soya beans, wheat, water and other aromatic ingredients, and is fermented for some months before being distilled.

When cooking, it is important to use the type of soy sauce specified in the recipe because the flavours are markedly different. For example, if you use light soy sauce when dark is specified, your dish might be too salty, or if you use dark instead of light the flavour of the soy sauce could be overpowering. In all my recipes, I use light soy sauce.

A WORLD OF FLAVOURS

SOY SAUCE

Scallop Salad, Oriental-style (page 72)

Scallop Salad, Oriental-style

Serves 4

- 12 fresh scallops (sea scallops), cleaned (without roe/coral)
- 2 tbsp light soy sauce
- 1 tsp each finely diced red and yellow sweet pepper
- 1 tsp finely diced courgette (zucchini)
- 1 tbsp vegetable oil
- 100 g/4 oz mixed salad leaves such as curly endive (frisée), oak leaf lettuce, radicchio, lollo rosso
- 12 tips of chicory (Belgian endive)
- fresh dill and coriander (cilantro) leaves, to garnish

Oriental dressing

- 2 tsp white wine vinegar
- 2 tsp walnut oil
- 2 tsp sunflower oil
- 1 pinch of finely chopped fresh hot chilli pepper
- 1 small carrot, peeled and grated
- 1 tsp fish gravy (nam pla)
- 1 tsp sugar
- 1 tsp chopped dried shrimps
- 1 medium-sized tomato, chopped
- salt and freshly ground white pepper

(Approximately 200 calories per portion)

This particular recipe is a first course that I devised for a very special state banquet held recently in The Dorchester Hotel. I was faced with the challenge of creating dishes that would appeal to our guests from the West and the East, and this succulent warm scallop salad pleased all palates. In it the scallops are marinated in soy sauce, which adds a full flavour to the dish and enhances the colour of the scallops when pan-fried. The nam pla (fish gravy or sauce) and dried shrimps are available from most Thai/Asian shops.

Scallops
Gently toss the scallops in the soy sauce to coat, then cover and place in the refrigerator to marinate.

Oriental dressing
Mix all the ingredients together and leave to stand for at least 1 hour. Strain the dressing through a fine sieve. Use a little to marinate the diced vegetables and keep the rest aside.

Scallops
Drain the scallops and pan-fry in the hot vegetable oil until medium cooked – approximately 2 minutes, depending on size. Remove from the pan, drain on paper towels, season and keep warm.

To Finish
Toss the salad leaves and chicory in the remaining oriental dressing. Use the chicory leaves to form a star shape on each plate. Put the remaining salad in the centre. Sprinkle the marinated diced vegetables around the salad. Place the scallops between the chicory. Garnish with herbs. Alternatively, to enhance the presentation, arrange the salad in a potato basket.

Red mullet with black beans and mashed potatoes

(Approximately 670 calories per portion)

This recipe has a definite Chinese influence in the black bean sauce. The soft mash accompanies the fish deliciously.

Mashed potatoes

Peel the potatoes, cut into chunks and place in a cooking pot. Cover with cold salted water, bring to the boil and simmer, covered, until cooked but slightly under-done. Drain in a colander and leave for 2-3 minutes to allow the water to evaporate, then press through a potato ricer into a larger saucepan. Place over low heat and, using a wooden spoon, mix in the butter cubes one by one. Heat the cream separately and then add to the potato mixture. Finally, season with salt, freshly ground pepper and a touch of nutmeg. Remove the pan from the heat, cover closely with buttered paper and keep warm.

Fish

Heat a non-stick pan, add the oil and slices of ginger, and sweat over medium heat for 1 minute. Add the seasoned fillets of red mullet, skin side down first, and brown very quickly on both sides. Remove the fillets from the pan and place in an ovenproof dish. Cover each of the fillets equally with the black bean sauce. Add the fish stock and cook in the preheated oven for 5-8 minutes, depending on the size of the fillets until the fish is cooked. Remove from the oven and keep aside.

To Finish

Pipe or spoon the mash potatoes into the centre of each plate and place 2 fillets of red mullet on top of the potato. Pour the cooking liquid left in the ovenproof dish over the fish, and garnish with dill, chervil and spring onion rings. Serve immediately.

Serves 4

1 tbsp vegetable oil
3 slices of fresh ginger, cut 3 mm/1/8 inch thick, peeled
8 red mullet fillets
4 tsp black bean sauce (see basic recipe, page 190), or use bought sauce
100 ml/4 fl oz fish stock (see basic recipe, page 190)

Mashed potatoes

4 medium-sized Desiree potatoes or another variety suitable for mashing
65 g/2 1/2 oz (5 tbsp) butter, at room temperature, cut into cubes
50 ml/2 fl oz single cream (light cream)
salt and freshly ground pepper
freshly grated nutmeg

Garnish

finely chopped fresh dill and chervil

1 spring onion (green onion), cut into fine rings

Oven temperature

200°C/400°F/Gas mark 6

Red Mullet with Black Beans and Mashed Potatoes
(page 73)

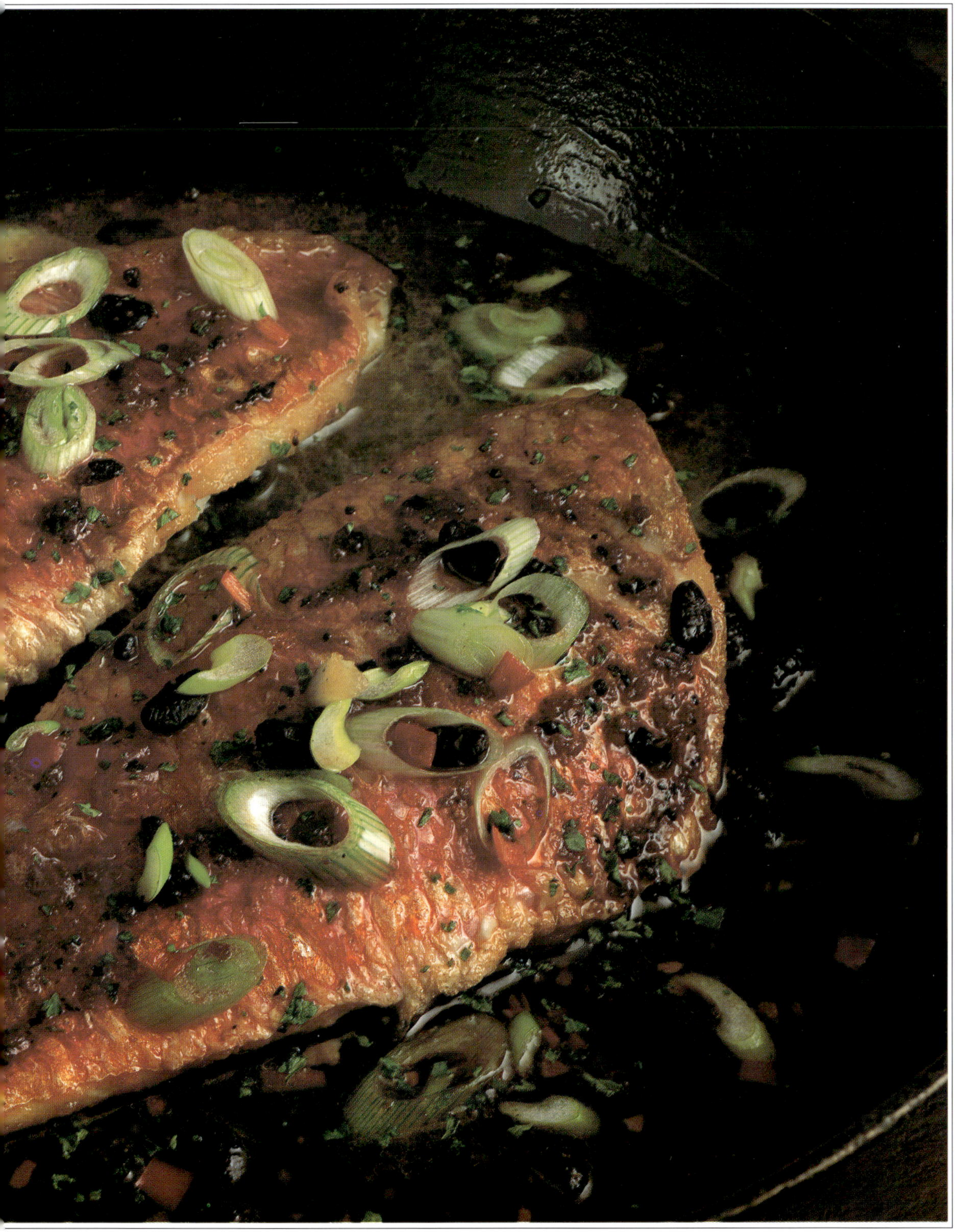

Broccoli and Cauliflower Timbale

Serves 4

Timbales

50 ml/2 fl oz clarified butter to brush the moulds
100 g/4 oz (1 cup) cauliflower, divided into small florets
100 g/4 oz (1 cup) broccoli, divided into small florets
3 eggs
2 egg yolks
100 ml/4 fl oz double cream (heavy cream)
50 ml/2 fl oz milk
salt and freshly ground white pepper
1 pinch of grated nutmeg, or to taste
8 medium-sized white asparagus spears
12 medium-sized green asparagus spears

Dressing

1 tsp light soy sauce
1 tsp coarse-grain mustard
4 tsp red wine vinegar
50 ml/2 fl oz sunflower oil
1 tsp walnut oil
½ tsp chopped fresh chervil

Garnish

100 g/4 oz mixed salad leaves, washed and dried
1 tsp chopped walnuts

You will need

4 timbale moulds, each about 6 cm/3 inches in diameter and 5 cm/2 ½ inches deep

Oven temperature

140°C/275°F/Gas mark 1

(Approximately 360 calories per portion)

This recipe takes time and care to prepare but makes an elegant first course for a dinner party.

Moulds

Place the timbale moulds in the freezer to chill. Whilst they are getting cold, cut 4 discs of greaseproof paper (wax paper) to fit the bottom of each mould. Then melt the clarified butter.

Now remove the moulds from the freezer and brush the inside of each with the butter, covering the surface well. Place a disc of paper on the bottom. Return the moulds to the refrigerator until required.

Timbales

Blanch the cauliflower and broccoli florets in boiling salted water for 3 minutes; they should still be crisp. Refresh immediately by plunging into a bowl of iced water and drain well. Remove the timbale moulds from the refrigerator and place the cauliflower and broccoli florets alternately into them. Arrange the florets face down and outwards, and close together. Fill the moulds three-quarters full, and press the florets down lightly with your fingertips. Keep to one side.

Beat the eggs and egg yolks lightly together. Whisk in the cream and milk. Season with salt, grated nutmeg and freshly ground white pepper, then strain into a small jug. Pour the mixture into the moulds, and cover each with heat-resistant film.

Place a couple of sheets of newspaper on the bottom of a roasting pan and stand the moulds on it. Pour enough boiling water into the pan to come about three-quarters up the moulds. Place in the lower part of the preheated oven and bake for about 1 hour 50 minutes or until cooked. To check if cooked, insert a small knife in the centre of a timbale, right to the bottom. If the knife comes out clean, the timbale is cooked. Keep an eye on the level of water as it may need topping up. Remove the timbales from oven and allow to cool.

Asparagus

Remove the woody base from each asparagus spear and peel the stalk if necessary. (These trimmings can be kept to make the stock for an asparagus soup, if you like.) Cook the prepared asparagus in boiling salted water. Drain, reserving 2 tsp of the cooking liquid, and refresh immediately by plunging into a bowl of iced water. Drain well and keep aside to garnish the timbales.

Dressing

Whisk all the ingredients thoroughly together with the reserved asparagus cooking liquid in a large bowl, or place in a jar, seal tightly with a lid and give it a good shake. Season to taste.

To Finish

Run a knife *very carefully* around the inside of each mould to loosen the timbale. Turn the moulds carefully upside down on a chopping board. Lift off the moulds, then gently transfer each timbale to a plate. Garnish with the cooked asparagus and salad leaves and sprinkle with the walnuts. Either serve the dressing separately or spoon it over the salad.

Barbecued Monkfish and Prawns with Aubergines and Plum Tomatoes

(Approximately 520 calories per portion)

An appetizing dish in which the warm vegetables, monkfish and prawns are served with a cold dressing. Any firm fish that is suitable for barbecuing or grilling can be substituted for the monkfish.

Dressing
Whisk all the ingredients together in a bowl, or place them in a jar, screw the lid on tightly and shake well. Keep aside.

Monkfish and prawns
Mix all the ingredients for the marinade together in a bowl. Add the prawns and the slices of monkfish and toss gently to coat. Cover and marinate in the refrigerator for about 30 minutes.

Drain the marinade from the prawns and fish. Keep it aside for cooking the aubergine.

Aubergine and tomato
Dust the aubergine slices with flour, shaking off any excess, then pat on gently. Brush each side with the marinade and season with salt and freshly ground pepper. Fry on both sides until golden brown. Remove from the pan, drain on paper towels and keep warm.

Put the remainder of the marinade in the pan and fry the tomato slices very quickly to warm through. Keep warm.

To Finish
Season the prawns and fish with salt and freshly ground pepper and barbecue, or cook them under a hot grill (broiler), until cooked but still moist inside, turning once.

Arrange the aubergine and tomato slices alternately in a large ring on 2 plates. Place the prawns and monkfish attractively in the centre and spoon over the dressing. Scatter the broad beans on top of the aubergines and tomato. To add a finishing touch, garnish with a few herbs, and serve.

Serves 2

6 raw king prawns (large shrimps), peeled and deveined
175 g/6 oz monkfish fillet, cut into 6 equal slices
1 medium-sized aubergine (egg plant), cut into 3 mm/1/8 inch slices
flour to dust aubergines
2 medium-sized plum tomatoes, peeled and cut into 3 mm/1/8 inch slices
10 shelled fresh broad beans (fava beans), cooked and peeled
fresh dill and chervil, to garnish

Dressing

1/2 tsp light soy sauce
1/2 shallot, peeled and finely chopped
1 tbsp white wine vinegar
1/2 lemon, juiced
3 tbsp olive oil
1 tbsp sunflower oil
salt and freshly ground pepper

Marinade for fish

1/2 lemon, juiced
5 tbsp vegetable oil
freshly ground white pepper
1 pinch of freshly ground cardamom

A WORLD OF FLAVOURS

Barbecued Monkfish and Prawns with Aubergines and Plum Tomatoes
(page 77)

SOY SAUCE

Chicken Salad with Roasted Garlic

Serves 4

- 100 g/4 oz white of leek
- 4 chicken breasts (breast halves)
- salt and freshly ground white pepper
- 50 ml/2 fl oz chicken stock (see basic recipe, page 190)
- 1 ½ tbsp dry sherry
- ½ tsp grated fresh ginger
- 1 small garlic clove, peeled and cut into thin slices
- 100 g/4 oz cucumber (English hot house cucumber), cut in half lengthwise and seeded
- ½ red sweet pepper, seeds removed, cut into 3 mm/⅛ inch dice
- 3 leaves of fresh coriander (cilantro), chopped
- 4 leaves of iceberg lettuce

Sauce

- 40 ml/1 ½ fl oz light soy sauce
- 2 tbsp white wine vinegar
- 25 g/1 oz (2 tbsp) white of leek, cut into 3 mm/⅛ inch dice
- 2 tbsp sesame oil
- ½ tsp grated fresh ginger

Oven temperature
180°C/350°F/Gas mark 4

(Approximately 220 calories per portion)

A substantial first course or light main course, this salad can be prepared well in advance and assembled just before eating.

Chicken

Trim the white part of the leek and remove the outer leaves. (Remember that you will need another 25 g/1 oz for the sauce.) Cut the piece of leek lengthwise into 4 and place in a greased ovenproof dish. Season the chicken breasts with salt and freshly ground white pepper and place on top of the leek.

Heat the chicken stock and sherry together until boiling and add the ginger. Pour over the chicken breasts and cover with a lid. Cook in the preheated oven for 15–20 minutes, turning once.

Remove the dish from the oven and allow the breasts to cool in the liquid. Then remove, and keep aside. Strain the liquid and keep aside for the sauce.

Sauce

Whilst the chicken breasts are cooking, prepare the sauce by mixing together all the ingredients for it.

Roasted Garlic

Place the slices of garlic on a small oiled baking tray and grill (broil) until golden. Allow to cool, then chop and keep aside.

To Finish

Add the cooking liquid from the chicken to the sauce. Remove the skin (and bone if necessary) from the breasts; cut each in half lengthwise and then across into fine strips. Cut the cucumber into strips about the same size and mix with the chicken. Add the diced red peppers and chopped coriander.

Carefully remove 4 leaves from an iceberg lettuce, ensuring that they remain 'cupped'. Wash and dry carefully. Place on serving dishes and divide the chicken salad among the 4 lettuce cups. Pour the sauce over and sprinkle with the roasted garlic.

Dublin Bay prawn broth

(Approximately 245 calories per portion)

A very simple but tasty soup that doesn't take a lot of effort to prepare.

Heat the vegetable oil in a medium-sized saucepan. Add the shallot, leek and carrots and sweat for about 2 minutes without colouring. Add the white wine and bring to the boil. Simmer for 2 minutes, then add the fish stock. Return to the boil and simmer until the vegetables are cooked but still a little crisp.

Add the soy sauce and season with salt and freshly ground pepper. Then add the Dublin Bay prawns and broad beans and stir very gently. Bring back to a simmer. Cover with a lid, remove from the heat and allow to rest for 3 minutes or until the prawns are cooked but not overcooked and tough.

To Finish
Spoon into soup bowls and garnish each with a sprig of dill and 2 wontons.

Serves 2

2 tbsp vegetable oil
1 shallot, peeled and finely sliced
1 small white of leek, cut into small rings
2 new carrots, peeled and cut into thin slices
100 ml/4 fl oz dry white wine
300 ml/10 fl oz fish stock (see basic recipe, page 190)
2 tbsp light soy sauce
salt and freshly ground pepper
6 raw Dublin Bay prawns in shell (without heads), cut lengthwise in half and deveined
10 shelled fresh broad beans (fava beans), quickly cooked in salt water, refreshed and peeled

Garnish

2 sprigs of fresh dill
4 filled wontons (bought from a Chinese supermarket), cooked

Salmon steak with celery and cashew nuts

(Approximately 425 calories per portion)

Cashew nuts are often used in Eastern cooking. Their crunchiness and flavour contrast surprisingly well with the delicate flesh of salmon.

Salmon
Heat the vegetable oil in a non-stick pan. Season the salmon steaks with salt and pepper and brown on both sides in the hot oil. Remove from the pan to an ovenproof dish. Keep aside.

Sauce
Mix the cornflour and English mustard with 4 tbsp of cold fish stock. Keep aside. Heat the vegetable oil in a saucepan. Sweat the celery, shallot and garlic until translucent, without colouring. Remove from the pan and keep aside.

Drain off any excess oil from the pan, then add the remaining fish stock and bring to the boil. Add the soy sauce. Add a little of the hot liquid to the cornflour mixture, then whisk it all back into the liquid in the pan. Bring back to the boil to thicken. Add the sweated vegetables and season with salt and pepper. Pour over the fish and cover the dish.

Bake in the preheated oven for about 10 minutes (depending on the size of steaks) or until the fish is cooked but still moist inside.

To Finish
Remove the dish from the oven. Spoon the sauce in the dish back over the fish. Sprinkle the spring onion rings, cashew nuts and chopped chives on top and serve.

Serves 2

1 tbsp vegetable oil
2 salmon steaks, each 150 g/5 oz
salt and freshly ground pepper

Sauce

¼ tsp cornflour (cornstarch)
1 pinch of English mustard powder
100 ml/4 fl oz fish stock (see basic recipe, page 190)
1 tbsp vegetable oil
1 celery stalk, 'strings' removed with a peeler, cut diagonally into 5 mm/¼ inch thick pieces
½ shallot, peeled and finely chopped
½ garlic clove, peeled and crushed with a knife or garlic press
1 tsp light soy sauce

Garnish

1 spring onion (green onion), cut into fine rings
8 cashew nuts, coarsely chopped and toasted under the grill (broiler)
2 tsp chopped fresh chives

Oven temperature

200°C/400°F/Gas mark 6

Barbecued sirloin steak with horseradish relish

(Approximately 740 calories per portion)

Japanese dips and sauces are the inspiration for this recipe, which I accompany with a selection of grilled vegetables.

Serves 4

2 tbsp vegetable oil
2 tbsp light soy sauce
freshly ground pepper
4 boneless sirloin steaks, each about 150 g/5 oz

Relish

4 tbsp mayonnaise
1 tbsp soy sauce
1 tbsp whole-grain mustard
2 tbsp bottled creamed horseradish
½ garlic clove, peeled and crushed with a knife or garlic press
1 spring onion (green onion), finely sliced
1 tbsp chopped parsley
salt and freshly ground pepper

Vegetables

1 small yellow sweet pepper, cut into quarters and seeds removed
1 small red sweet pepper, cut into quarters and seeds removed
1 medium-sized green courgette (zucchini), cut into 4 pieces lengthwise
1 medium-sized yellow courgette (yellow zucchini), cut into 4 pieces lengthwise
2 tbsp vegetable oil

Marinade
Mix together the vegetable oil, soy sauce and pepper. Add the sirloin steaks and marinate for 30 minutes.

Relish
Whilst the steaks are marinating, mix together all the ingredients for the relish and season with salt and freshly ground pepper. Keep to one side.

Vegetables
Brush the vegetables with the oil and season with salt and pepper. Either barbecue the peppers, followed by the courgettes, or bake in a preheated oven (170°C/325°F/Gas mark 3) – the peppers will take about 10 minutes and the courgettes 5 minutes. Place in a serving dish and keep warm.

To Finish
Char-grill the steaks on the barbecue or, if you prefer, pan-fry in a hot non-stick pan. First brown on each side, seasoning with salt and freshly ground pepper, then reduce the heat and continue cooking for about 5 minutes, depending on size, until medium cooked. Remove from the heat and allow to rest for 3–4 minutes in a warm place.

Place the steaks on top of the char-grilled vegetables and serve the relish separately.

Creamy glazed chicken legs

(Approximately 415 calories per portion)

Serves 2

1 tbsp vegetable oil
2 chicken leg portions
freshly ground pepper
1 tbsp flour to dust chicken
50 ml/2 fl oz white wine
½ lime, juiced
1 tsp light soy sauce
1 pinch of English mustard powder
½ tsp curry powder
150 ml/5 fl oz single cream (light cream)

Oven temperature

180°C/350°F/Gas mark 4

Chicken
Heat the oil in a non-stick pan. Using a piece of paper towel, pat the chicken legs dry and season with pepper. Dust with flour, then shake off any excess. Brown the chicken legs on both sides in the hot oil, and remove to an ovenproof dish.

Sauce
Pour the remaining oil from the pan, then add the white wine and bring to the boil. Add the lime juice, soy sauce, mustard and curry powder and boil for 1 minute. Add the cream and simmer over a low heat for about 2 minutes. Season with pepper.

Pour the sauce over the chicken, cover with a lid and bake in the lower part of the preheated oven for about 20 minutes.

To Finish
Remove the chicken from the sauce and place it on a baking tray. Bake the chicken for a further 10 minutes. Pour the sauce into a saucepan, gently reheat and, if necessary, adjust the seasoning. Serve with the chicken.

Cinnamon

Although I have used cinnamon in sweet dishes for as long as I can remember, I discovered in Sri Lanka that it has an extraordinary versatility. It is the dried bark of a tropical tree, and is commonly found both in powdered form and as rolled 'sticks'. It should not be confused with cassia, the dried bark of a different tree, with a similar flavour and smell to cinnamon, that is usually sold in fragments.

In my early years as a chef, I worked in a hotel in Switzerland which regularly put on culinary events with other leading hotels all over the world. Every time we had such an event, I used to collect one of the unusual spices or ingredients and put them into jars. In this way, I built up my own library of ingredients. One of the hotels invited to participate was in Sri Lanka, and they sent not only their chefs, who brought with them their own special ingredients, but also their musicians!

One of the ingredients the Sri Lankan chefs used liberally was cinnamon. We, of course, used cinnamon too, but normally only in sweet dishes. However, one of the chefs, Dazza, showed me that cinnamon has much more to offer than I had ever believed. It can be used with lamb and fish, in curries and rice dishes, in breads, to preserve fruits, in pickles and soups, and even in hot drinks.

Many years later, I had the opportunity to travel around the Eden of Sri Lanka - an absolutely amazing experience. The visit was made particularly memorable due to my acquaintance with Chef Dazza, who dedicated a lot of time to showing me his country. We started our exploration in Colombo, in his ancient Mini Minor with tyres that were completely bald. (We certainly paid the price for these, with at least three punctures along the way, but it didn't matter - it only added more excitement to the journey.) We passed Negombo, where we watched the fishermen coming in from the sea with their catches, including some beautiful crayfish. Driving on to Nuwara Eliya, we passed some of the best tea plantations in the world. Here, we were shown how the top three leaves of each plant are picked by the skilful hands of the Tamil women and then processed. That night, Dazza dropped me off at the Hills Club, a relic from the days of the British Empire. Here, I was temporarily embarrassed - my luggage didn't include the requisite tie! Luckily the charming host lent me one of his, and a jacket, which was two or three sizes too small and which I wore with a polo-style T-shirt. But at least I conformed to the rules of the house. Despite my unorthodox dress I had a lovely dinner, and the atmosphere of the club made for a fascinating evening.

The highlight of the trip was a visit to a spice garden, where I could see fresh and growing all the spices that I had previously only seen in their dried form – vanilla pods, which are the fruit of a beautifully coloured orchid; the seeds or beans of the evergreen cacao tree, from which chocolate and cocoa powder are produced; nutmeg in its lacy membrane (when dried this is mace), which is found inside the fruit of an evergreen tree; grape-like clusters of peppercorns hanging from their plants; star anise; and, of course, cinnamon, which is the inner bark of a tree native to Sri Lanka. A dream come true! What an education!

It was especially fascinating to see how cinnamon is produced. The trees are pruned hard to produce a maximum number of branches, and to ease harvesting which takes place during the rainy season when the bark is more pliable. Then the outer bark is pulled back and the outer skin is scraped off the inner bark, leaving pale brown strips. These are dried, curling into long quills. Successive harvests reap better quality bark, the finest being the thinnest from the tender shoots at the centre of the tree.

The woody aroma from the dried cinnamon bark is intense yet sweet and delicate. This is why the essential oil is much used in aromatherapy: if you have a cold, inhaling a little cinnamon oil will clear your head. The taste of cinnamon is one that we are all familiar with, and can lend itself to a diverse range of dishes, as Dazza showed me so many years ago.

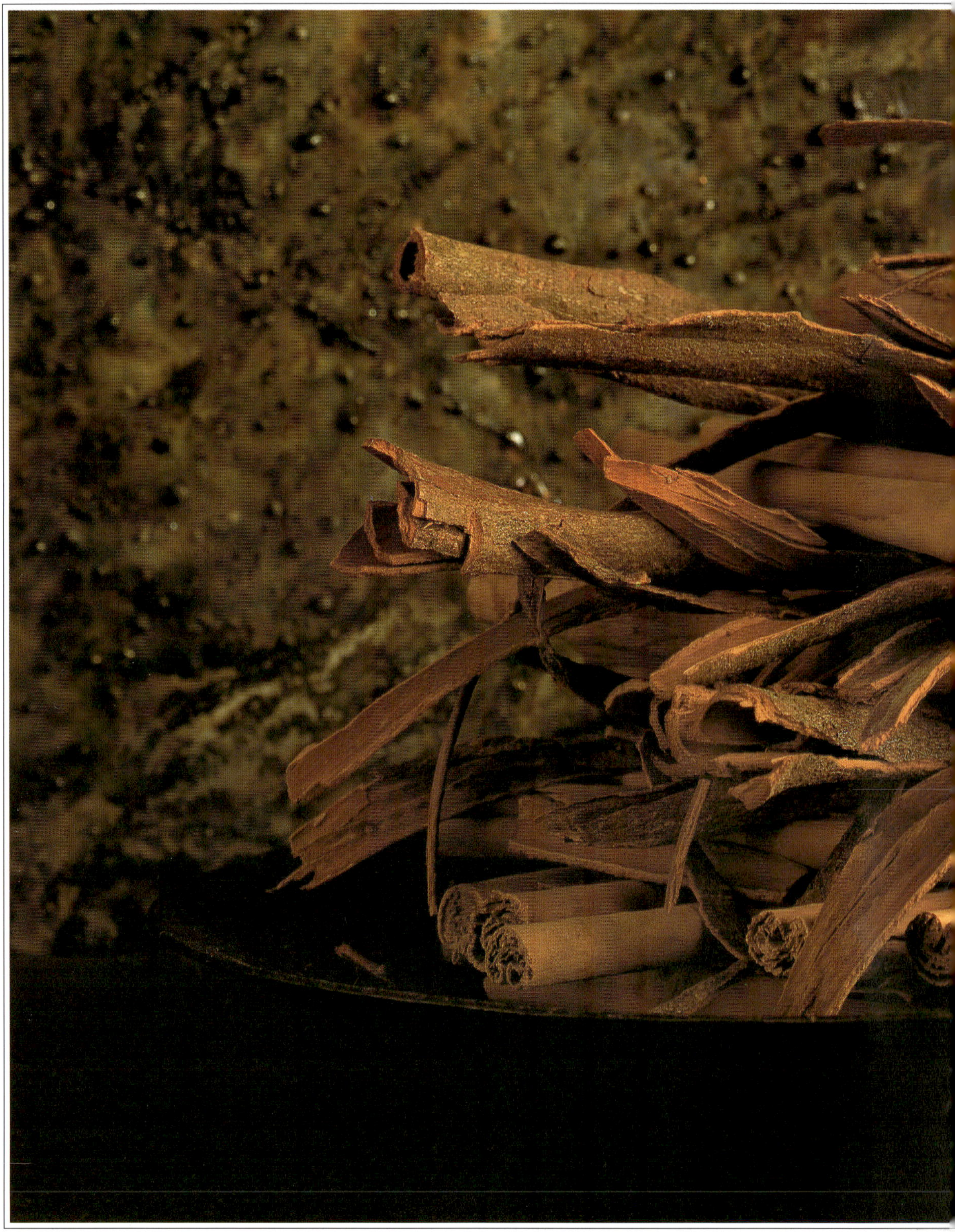

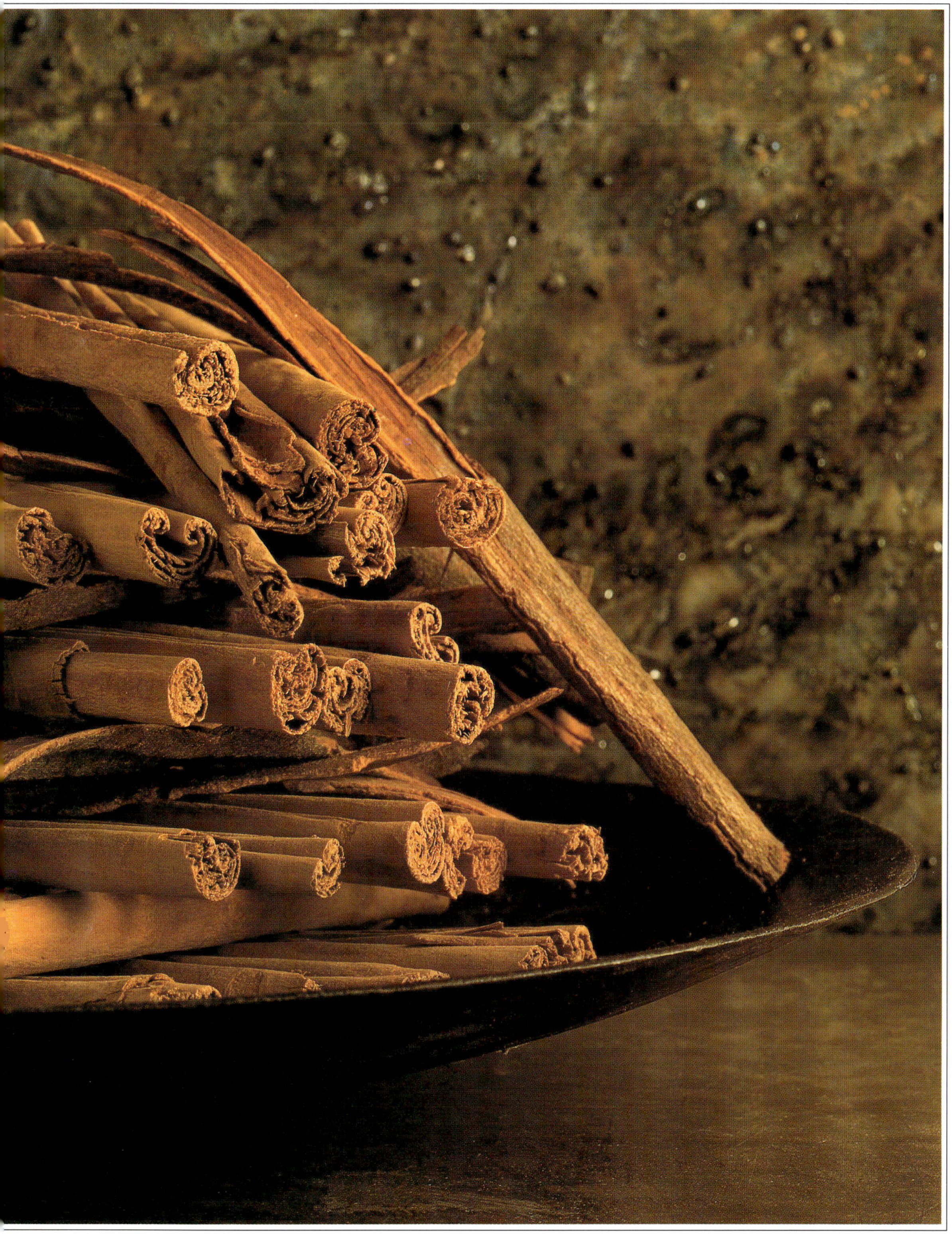

Celeriac and Chestnut Soup

Serves 4

200 g/7 oz chestnuts
2 tbsp caster sugar (granulated sugar)
1 lt/1 ¾ pt (1 qt) vegetable stock (see basic recipe, page 193)
2 tbsp vegetable oil
2 shallots, peeled and sliced
1 garlic clove, peeled and crushed with a knife or garlic press
1 small carrot, peeled and cut into thumb-sized pieces
200 g/7 oz celeriac (celery root), peeled and cut into thumb-sized pieces
1 cinnamon stick
100 g/4 oz (⅔ cup) peeled potatoes, cut into thumb-sized pieces
100 ml/4 fl oz single cream (light cream)
2 tbsp chopped fresh chives

Oven temperature
200°C/400°F/Gas mark 6

(Approximately 260 calories per portion)

A real winter warmer! The recipe calls for fresh chestnuts, but you can also use canned. Just omit the first step as canned chestnuts are already cooked.

Chestnuts

Using a sharp knife, make a criss-cross incision through the base of each chestnut. Place them on a baking tray and roast in the preheated oven for about 10 minutes. Remove from the oven, peel off the skin and husk, and chop the chestnuts coarsely. Keep aside. Put the sugar into a saucepan and place over medium heat. Heat slowly, without stirring, until the sugar is golden brown. Remove from the heat. Add the chopped chestnuts and about 100 ml/4 fl oz of the cold vegetable stock. Bring to the boil and simmer for 5 minutes.

Soup

Meanwhile, heat the vegetable oil in a large saucepan, add the shallots, garlic, carrot and celeriac, and sweat gently for 2–3 minutes without colouring. Add the sugar and chestnut mixture and the cinnamon stick and bring to the boil. Add the remaining cold vegetable stock and bring back to the boil. Add the potatoes and simmer for about 30 minutes. When the potatoes are cooked, remove the cinnamon stick and allow the mixture to cool slightly. Then, using a hand blender or a food processor, purée the mixture, and pass it through a sieve into a clean saucepan.

To Finish

When ready to eat, bring the soup back to the boil. Add the cream, adjust the seasoning if necessary, and simmer for 2 minutes. Add the chopped chives and serve.

Red Lentil and Clam Soup

(Approximately 210 calories per portion)

A hearty soup for a chilly day! The lentils are soaked overnight to speed up the cooking process, but this is not essential, so if you don't have the time to wait just double the cooking time and test that the lentils are soft before proceeding.

Serves 4

75 g/3 oz (6 tbsp) red lentils
2 tbsp vegetable oil
200 g/7 oz fresh clams, washed and rinsed
2 shallots, peeled and finely chopped
1 garlic clove, peeled and crushed with a knife or garlic press
1 cinnamon stick
1 tsp mild curry powder
100 ml/4 fl oz white wine
1 lt/1 3/4 pt (1 qt) fish stock (see basic recipe, page 190)
100 ml/4 fl oz single cream (light cream)
salt and freshly ground pepper
1 tsp finely chopped fresh basil

Cover the lentils with water and leave to soak overnight. The next day drain, rinse and keep aside.

Clams

Heat the vegetable oil in a saucepan large enough to hold all the clams. Add the clams and cook for 1 minute. Add the shallots, garlic, cinnamon stick and curry powder and cook for a further minute. Pour in the white wine and bring to the boil. Cover with a lid and simmer until the clams are open. Remove the clams with a slotted spoon and keep aside. (Discard any clams that remain closed.)

Soup

Add the red lentils to the cooking liquid. Add the fish stock, bring to the boil and simmer for about 30 minutes or until the lentils are soft.

Whilst the lentils are cooking, remove the clams from the shells and keep aside. Discard the shells.

When the lentils are tender, remove the cinnamon stick and allow the soup to cool slightly. Then use a hand blender or food processor to purée the soup. Pour the soup into a saucepan and bring back to the boil. Add the cream and season with salt and freshly ground pepper.

To Finish

When ready to eat, return the soup to the boil and simmer for 2 minutes. Remove from the heat, add the clams and chopped basil and serve.

Tomato Bredie

Serves 4

1 tbsp vegetable oil
800 g/1 ¾ lb boneless shoulder of lamb, cut into thumb-sized cubes
salt and freshly ground pepper
2 onions, peeled and finely chopped
2 garlic cloves, peeled
1 tsp brown sugar
1 bay leaf
½ tsp mild curry powder
2 cinnamon sticks
1 pinch of cayenne pepper
100 ml/4 fl oz lamb stock (see basic recipe, page 192)
5 large tomatoes, peeled and coarsely chopped
3 medium-sized potatoes, peeled and cut into thumb-sized pieces

Oven temperature
170°C/325°F/Gas mark 3

(Approximately 500 calories per portion)

I first tasted this rich and flavourful dish when it was cooked by Graham Morrison in a traditional caste-iron 'potjie' over an open fire. In its original form the bredie would have been even richer, made from lambs' tails. Graham's dish was so good that I've endeavoured to recreate it here. I like to serve this with Mandoub's rice (see page 189).

Heat the vegetable oil in a non-stick pan. Season the lamb with salt and freshly ground pepper. When the oil is hot, add about 6–8 lamb cubes and brown on all sides. Using a slotted spoon, transfer the cubes to an ovenproof dish. Repeat the process until all the lamb is browned.

Using the same non-stick pan, sweat the onions and garlic with the brown sugar until translucent, without colouring. Add the bay leaf, curry powder, cinnamon sticks and cayenne pepper. Add the lamb stock and tomatoes and bring to the boil. Pour over the meat in the ovenproof dish and cover with a lid. Place in the preheated oven and simmer for about 1 hour.

Add the potatoes, replace the lid and cook for a further 25 minutes or until the meat and potatoes are cooked.

To Finish

Remove the cinnamon stick and bay leaf. Finally, check the seasoning and serve.

Lamb and Okra Hotpot

Serves 2

200 g/7 oz boneless lamb (neck or shoulder), cut into 2.5 cm/1 inch cubes
300 ml/10 fl oz water
¼ onion, peeled
1 garlic clove, peeled and crushed with a knife or garlic press
1 piece of cinnamon stick, 1 cm/½ inch long
2 whole cardamom pods, or 1 pinch of ground cardamom
¼ bay leaf

Sauce

1 tbsp vegetable oil
¾ onion, peeled and finely chopped
1 garlic clove, peeled and crushed with a knife or garlic press
150 g/5 oz okra, tops removed
1 pinch of ground ginger
¼ tsp turmeric
1 pinch of chilli powder
¼ tsp mild curry powder
2 tbsp plain yoghurt

(Approximately 395 calories per portion)

Although not difficult to prepare, this lamb stew does take some time to cook. This allows the flavours to combine deliciously and is well worth the wait.

Lamb

Place the lamb cubes in a saucepan together with the cold water. Bring to the boil and skim off any impurities. Add the onion, garlic, cinnamon stick, cardamom and bay leaf. Cover with a lid and simmer gently for about 1 ¼ hours. Strain off the liquid, reserving it for the sauce. Keep the lamb cubes aside.

Sauce

Heat the oil in a saucepan large enough to hold the meat and the remaining liquid. Add the onion and garlic and sweat until translucent, without colouring. Add the okra and sweat for a further 5 minutes. Add the ginger, turmeric, chilli, curry powder and yoghurt and bring to the boil. Add the meat and the strained cooking liquid. Simmer for a further 15–20 minutes or until the meat is tender.

To Finish

When the meat is cooked, check the seasoning and adjust if necessary. Serve hot.

Monkfish with Beansprouts and Mangetout

(Approximately 410 calories per portion)

I first came across cinnamon being used to flavour fish whilst watching a local woman cook in Bali. She let me taste the dish and I was struck by how unusual and pleasant the result was.

Mangetout
Top and tail the mangetout, then drop them into boiling salted water and simmer for 3 minutes. Immediately plunge them into a bowl of iced water to refresh, then drain and keep to one side.

Sauce
Sweat the shallot and cinnamon stick in the butter until the shallot is translucent, without colouring. Remove the cinnamon stick. Add the brandy and white wine, bring to the boil and simmer to reduce to half the quantity. Then add the fish stock, return to the boil and simmer to reduce to half the quantity again. Add the cream and boil until a creamy consistency is obtained.

Pass the sauce through a sieve into a clean saucepan and season with salt and freshly ground white pepper. Keep to one side.

Fish
About 15 minutes before eating, prepare the fish. Season the slices of monkfish with salt and freshly ground white pepper, then coat with flour, shaking off any excess. (I find the easiest way to do this is to place the flour in a plastic bag, add the fish pieces and shake gently to coat.) Heat the sunflower oil in a non-stick pan.

Add the monkfish to the pan and fry over medium heat for about 2–3 minutes or until golden brown on both sides. Remove from the pan and place in an ovenproof dish. Bake in the preheated oven for 8 minutes or until cooked.

Vegetables
Whilst the fish is in the oven, heat the butter in a non-stick pan and add the mangetout. Stir-fry for a few seconds, then add the beansprouts and stir-fry for 30 seconds. Add the diced tomato. Season with salt and freshly ground white pepper.

To Finish
When the fish is cooked, remove it from the oven and place on a warm serving dish. Bring the sauce to the boil and pour it over the fish. Sprinkle the vegetables on top and serve immediately.

Serves 4

200 g/7 oz small mangetout (snow peas)
800 g/1 ¾ lb monkfish fillets, cut into 2 cm/¾ inch slices
salt and freshly ground white pepper
flour to coat the fish
2 tbsp sunflower oil
25 g/1 oz (2 tbsp) butter
200 g/7 oz (2 cups) beansprouts
1 small tomato, peeled, seeded and diced

Sauce

25 g/1 oz (2 tbsp) chopped shallot
1 piece of cinnamon stick, 1 cm/½ inch long
25 g/1 oz (2 tbsp) unsalted butter
2 tsp brandy
50 ml/2 fl oz dry white wine
100 ml/4 fl oz fish stock (see basic recipe, page 190)
150 ml/5 fl oz double cream (heavy cream)

Oven temperature

170°C/325°F/Gas mark 3

Chicken with Cinnamon Sauce

Serves 4

2 tbsp vegetable oil
4 chicken leg portions (drumstick and thigh)
salt and freshly ground white pepper
flour to dust the chicken

Sauce

2 tbsp vegetable oil
1 shallot, peeled and finely chopped
1 garlic clove, peeled and crushed with a knife or garlic press
1 cinnamon stick
1 red sweet pepper, seeds removed, cut into cubes
1 green sweet pepper, seeds removed, cut into cubes
1 orange, juiced
150 ml/5 fl oz chicken stock (see basic recipe, page 190)
1 tsp mild paprika
200 ml/7 fl oz single cream (light cream)
1 tsp cornflour (cornstarch)

Oven temperature
180°C/350°F/Gas mark 4

(Approximately 390 calories per portion)

In Sri Lanka, my eyes were opened to the versatility of cinnamon. Later, working alongside Noreen Scott, my Malaysian chef, I learnt that this spice is also used widely in Eastern cooking, which further encouraged me to experiment with it.

Chicken

Heat the oil in a non-stick pan. Season the chicken legs and dust with flour, shaking off any excess. Then add to the pan and brown on both sides. Remove to a fairly large ovenproof dish. Bake in the preheated oven for 10 minutes.

Sauce

In the meantime, prepare the sauce. Heat the oil in a saucepan and sweat the shallot and garlic with the cinnamon stick until the shallots are translucent, without colouring. Add red and green pepper pieces and sweat for a further minute. Add the orange juice and bring to the boil. Reserve 50 ml/2 fl oz of the chicken stock for later; add the remainder to the saucepan with the paprika. Return to the boil. Pour the sauce over the chicken. Cover with a lid, return to the oven and bake for a further 20 minutes.

Remove the chicken from the oven and pierce the thickest part of the drumstick with a needle. If the juices running out are clear, the chicken is cooked. If not, return to the oven.

To Finish

When they are cooked, remove the chicken legs from the sauce and keep warm in a serving dish. Discard the cinnamon stick and pour the sauce into a saucepan. Add the cream and boil for about 3 minutes. Skim off the fat. Season with salt and pepper.

Mix the cornflour with the reserved cold chicken stock. Add a little of the hot sauce to it, then whisk this into the sauce in the pan. Bring to the boil and simmer for a few minutes. Pour over the chicken and serve.

Roast Pheasant with Apple and Papaya

(Approximately 390 calories per portion)

During my apprenticeship, my chef always bought game birds in with feathers. I was then despatched to the cellar, to sit at a table piled high with the birds to be plucked. Sometimes this task took me until well past midnight - and even then the birds followed me into my dreams!

Today things are different, and we are able to buy pheasant (and other game birds too) plucked and cleaned. But old habits die hard, and I still prefer to buy birds with their feather on, and to mature them myself.

Pheasant

Heat the oil in a roasting pan and quickly brown the pheasant on all sides. Then season and turn breast up in the pan. Add the stick of cinnamon. Roast in the preheated oven, basting frequently, until cooked but still pink. This will take 25-30 minutes, depending on the size of the bird.

Sauce

Whilst the pheasant is in the oven, prepare the sauce. Heat the vegetable oil in a saucepan and sweat the shallot and garlic until translucent, without colouring. Add the papaya and apple pieces and sweat for a further minute, then add the chicken stock and bring to the boil. Cover with a lid and simmer for 5 minutes.

Allow the mixture to cool slightly, then purée in a food processor and pass through a sieve into a clean pan. Add the vinegar and season with salt and pepper.

To Finish

When the pheasant is cooked, remove it from the roasting pan and allow it to rest in a warm place for about 10 minutes. To facilitate carving, remove the wishbone. Then carve the bird and place it on a serving dish. Bring the sauce to the boil, and serve it separately.

Serves 2

- 2 tbsp vegetable oil
- 1 pheasant, cleaned
- salt and freshly ground pepper
- 1 piece of cinnamon stick, 2 cm/¾ inch long

Sauce

- 1 tbsp vegetable oil
- ½ shallot, peeled and finely chopped
- ¼ garlic clove, peeled and crushed with a knife of garlic press
- ¼ ripe papaya, peeled, seeded and cut into small pieces
- ¼ Golden Delicious apple, peeled, cored and cut into small pieces
- 150 ml/5 fl oz chicken stock (see basic recipe, page 190)
- 1 tsp white wine vinegar

Oven temperature

180 °C/350°F/Gas mark 4

A WORLD OF FLAVOURS

CINNAMON

Ricotta
Cheesecake
(page 96)

Ricotta Cheesecake

Serves 4

250 g/9 oz sweet pastry (see basic recipe, page 195)

flour to dust pastry

Filling

300 g/11 oz (1 ⅓ cups) ricotta cheese

50 g/2 oz caster sugar (¼ cup granulated sugar)

25 g/1 oz (2 tbsp) candied orange peel, diced

25 g/1 oz milk chocolate, diced

1 egg, lightly beaten; reserve 2 tsp for glazing the pastry

¼ tsp ground cinnamon

pure vanilla essence (vanilla extract) to taste

¼ lime, juiced

½ tsp grated orange zest

To serve

icing sugar (confectioners' sugar)

4 sprigs of fresh mint

sauce anglaise (see basic recipe, page 195)

peach sorbet

50 ml/2 fl oz chocolate sauce (see basic recipe, page 194 – optional)

You will need

4 tartlet moulds, each 10 cm/4 inches in diameter

Oven temperature

180°C/350°F/Gas mark 4

(Approximately 620 calories per portion)

A delightful sweet, this is best served slightly warm, with a scoop of peach sorbet.

Pastry

Dust the pastry dough lightly with flour and roll out to about 3 mm/⅛ inch thick. Use to line the tartlet moulds and allow to rest for 20 minutes. Cut the remaining pastry dough into 24 strips, each 5 mm/¼ inch wide and approximately 10 cm/4 inches long. Keep aside to make a lattice top finish.

Filling

Combine all the ingredients in a bowl (remember to keep aside 2 tsp of the beaten egg) and beat well. Divide the mixture equally among the 4 tartlet cases. Use 6 pastry strips to form a lattice pattern on top of each tartlet, trimming off the excess pastry. Use a pastry brush to gently brush the lattice strips with the reserved lightly beaten egg. Bake in the preheated oven for 25–30 minutes.

Remove from the oven and cool on a wire rack for 5 minutes. Then remove from the moulds and allow to cool further on the rack. As they cool, the filling will 'relax' and shrink a little.

To Finish

Serve slightly warm, dusted with icing sugar and garnished with a sprig of mint, with the sauce anglaise and a scoop of peach sorbet.

Alternatively, to give an extra artistic touch, ladle some sauce anglaise into the centre of each plate to form a disc about 10 cm/4 inches in diameter. Put the chocolate sauce into a paper piping bag, cut a very small hole in the end, and pipe a thin line around the edge of the sauce anglaise. Then, using a cocktail stick, swirl the chocolate through the sauce anglaise in a circular motion to make a pattern. Set a tartlet on the sauce for serving.

Cinnamon and Fig Gratin

(Approximately 290 calories per portion)

Some of the best figs I've ever tasted were on a boat leaving the Greek islands behind me on my way to Turkey. Whilst figs are delicious eaten fresh, they can also be enjoyed hot, as in this gratin.

Ice-cream
Soften the vanilla ice-cream slightly and place in a bowl. Add some cinnamon and mix with a wooden spoon. Keep in the freezer until required.

Figs
Cut each fig into quarters. Keep aside.

Place the sugar, red wine, water and cinnamon stick in a saucepan and bring to the boil. Simmer for 2 minutes. Add the figs, making sure that they are covered with liquid, and remove from heat. Cover with a lid and allow to cool.

Remove the figs from the liquid and place in a flameproof dish. Keep aside. Bring the cooking liquid to the boil and boil to reduce to half the quantity. Reserve 1 tbsp for the gratin mixture, and pour the rest over the figs.

Gratin mixture
Just before serving, whisk together all the ingredients (including the 1 tbsp liquid from the figs) in a metal bowl. Set the bowl over a saucepan of almost simmering water and continue whisking until the mixture is thick and foamy but not too 'runny'. Pour it over the figs immediately.

To Finish
Place the dish under the preheated grill (broiler) and bake until golden brown. Using a fine sieve, dust icing sugar over the top and garnish with mint. Serve instantly, with the ice-cream.

Serves 4

12 fresh figs
50 g/2 oz (¼ cup) sugar
100 ml/4 fl oz red wine
50 ml/2 fl oz water
1 cinnamon stick

Gratin mixture

4 egg yolks (freeze the egg whites for another dish)
2 tbsp sugar
4 tbsp single cream (light cream)
½ tsp grated orange zest

To serve

vanilla ice-cream
a little ground cinnamon
icing sugar (confectioners' sugar)
fresh mint

Grill (broiler)

medium hot

*Cinnamon and
Fig Gratin
(page 97)*

CINNAMON

Poached Pear with Cinnamon

Serves 4

- 4 ripe William's pears (US Bartlett pears)
- fresh mint, to garnish
- vanilla ice-cream, to serve (optional)

Syrup
- 375 ml/13 fl oz red wine
- 50 ml/2 fl oz port wine
- grated zest and juice of 1 lemon
- grated zest and juice of ½ orange
- 2 cloves
- 1 cinnamon stick
- 2 pieces of star anise
- 1 bay leaf
- 175 g/6 oz caster sugar (US ¾ cup granulated sugar)
- 150 ml/5 fl oz water
- 1 tbsp cornflour (US cornstarch), mixed with 2 tbsp water

(Approximately 290 calories per portion)

Syrup
Combine all the ingredients for the syrup (except the cornflour) in a saucepan large enough to hold the pears. Bring slowly to the boil and simmer for 10 minutes.

Pears
Meanwhile, using a vegetable peeler, carefully peel the pears, leaving the stalks intact. Holding each pear upside down, gently remove the core and seeds, working from the base. When the syrup is ready, add the pears and return to the boil. Cover with a lid and simmer very gently until cooked, approximately 40–50 minutes. Turn the pears during cooking to ensure an even colour. To check that the pears are cooked, pierce with a knife to make sure they are tender. Remove the saucepan from the heat and allow the pears to cool in the syrup.

Remove the pears very gently with a slotted spoon and place in a serving dish. Strain the cooking liquid into a clean saucepan and bring to the boil. Whisking vigorously, add the cornflour mixture to the liquid. Return to the boil and simmer to thicken. Allow to cool.

To Finish
Spoon a little sauce over the pears to make them shine. Garnish with mint, and serve ice-cream separately.

Pumpkin and Coconut Cake

Makes 1 cake/12 slices

- 300 g/11 oz (1 ½ cups) peeled pumpkin, roughly chopped
- 100 g/4 oz sultanas (⅔ cup golden raisins)
- 2 tbsp brandy
- 250 g/9 oz (1 cup+2 tbsp) unsalted butter, at room temperature
- 175 g/6 oz caster sugar (¾ cup granulated sugar)
- 2 eggs, lightly beaten
- 50 g/2 oz desiccated coconut (½ cup unsweetened dried shredded coconut)
- 100 ml/4 fl oz milk
- 325 g/12 oz self-raising flour (2 ½ cups self-raising flour)
- 1 tsp ground cinnamon
- 1 pinch of salt
- 100 g/4 oz (⅔ cup) candied orange peel, finely chopped
- icing sugar (confectioners' sugar), to garnish

You will need
a round loose-bottomed cake pan, 24 cm/9 ½ inches in diameter

Oven temperature
170°C/325°F/Gas mark 3

(Approximately 400 calories per portion)

A moist and fruity tea cake which can also be served as a dessert. I like it slightly warm with honey ice-cream and orange sauce (see page 194).

Pan
Line the bottom and sides of the cake pan with greaseproof paper (wax paper). Grease lightly.

Cook the pumpkin in boiling water until tender. Drain, mash and allow to cool. Keep aside. Soak the sultanas in the brandy. Keep aside.

Cake mixture
Beat the butter with the sugar until smooth and creamy. Add the eggs a little at a time, then add the coconut. Add half the milk and half the flour to the mixture and mix until smooth, then add the remaining milk and flour. Add the cinnamon and salt. Finally, fold in the soaked sultanas, orange peel and pumpkin.

Spoon the mixture into the pan and smooth the top with a wet palette knife (metal spatula). Bake in the preheated oven for approximately 1 hour. To test if cooked, insert a small knife or skewer in the centre; it should come out clean.

Remove from the oven and allow to rest for 15 minutes before removing from the pan. Cool on a rack. Sprinkle icing sugar on top before serving.

Sesame Oil

The seeds of the sesame plant have been crushed for their oil for thousands of years. Two kinds of oil are available: light-coloured, cold-pressed oil, and the dark, thick, powerfully aromatic oil from toasted seeds – indispensable in Eastern cooking – that I prefer to use. Sesame oil burns easily and so for frying it is often mixed with another oil. In Oriental cooking it is generally added as a final flavouring ingredient.

A WORLD OF FLAVOURS

SESAME OIL

My one visit to Burma was quite short, due to visa restrictions, but nevertheless it was memorable and full of contrasts.

After many early starts to queue in vain at Mandalay airport to get a ticket to Pagan, I eventually was successful, and got a seat on an old two-engined propeller plane, a Fokker. The ensuing 1 1/2 hour flight was a hair-raising experience, and at the end I was extremely glad to feel firm ground underneath my feet again.

On arrival, I found accommodation at the 'Bamboo Guest House'. As its name implied, it was made entirely of bamboo, and in the heat of the day a welcome breeze came through the slats to cool the hot room. What more could I have asked for – a room with air conditioning, a luxury I couldn't have afforded otherwise. But at night it was a different story – I couldn't adjust the slats and it was freezing cold. So, by the light of a candle, I had to put on all the clothes I had with me, including an anorak, in an attempt to keep warm. In the morning, the owner took pity on me and gave me a cup of hot Chinese tea. It felt like a gift from heaven.

Later, travelling at the back of a small bus, I found myself at the idyllic Lake Inle. A strange feeling came over me there, a feeling difficult to describe, but almost as if I were on a different planet. The scenery was unforgettably beautiful: bare, perfectly shaped mountains reflected in the crystal clear waters of the lake. I quickly found a boatman willing to take me out on the lake. His boat was hand-carved from a tree trunk, and he propelled it very skilfully using only an arm and a leg.

The lake was full of islands of delightfully scented hyacinths and amazing floating gardens where tomatoes and potatoes grew. The boatman left me at a Buddhist monastery built on stilts, where I received a warm welcome from the monks. Their heads were cleanly shaven and their bodies wrapped in yellow or bright orange red robes. They showed me around the monastery, including the kitchen with its open fire and huge cooking pot. A monk was preparing a bala chuang – the pungent shrimp paste relish that the Burmese consider essential on the table.

Bala chuang contains sesame oil, as do many other Burmese dishes. Extracted from sesame seeds, this oil is thick, rich and golden brown and has a wonderful nutty taste and aroma. It is also widely used in China, Korea and Japan to season and to intensify other flavours.

Sesame oil heats rapidly and burns easily, so when used for frying it is normally mixed with another oil. I found out many years after my Burma trip from Tony, one of my Chinese chefs, that many people like to add a dash of sesame oil to a dish at the last moment, as a final seasoning. I often use sesame oil in cooking, and I also like to add it to salad dressings. I use the seeds, both black and white, as a garnish, or mixed with breadcrumbs for coating fish and meat.

A WORLD OF FLAVOURS

*Baked Salmon
in Lotus Leaves
(page 108)*

SESAME OIL

Baked Salmon in Lotus Leaves

Serves 2

2 lotus leaves
1 tbsp sesame oil
2 salmon steaks, each about 200 g/7 oz
salt and freshly ground pepper
2 shallots, peeled and sliced
1 red sweet pepper, seeds removed, cut into strips
1 yellow sweet pepper, seeds removed, cut into strips
1 garlic clove, peeled and crushed with a knife or garlic press
3 fresh shiitake mushrooms, cut into quarters
finely chopped mixed fresh green herbs, to garnish

Oven temperature

180°C/350°F/Gas mark 4

(Approximately 460 calories per portion)

I got the idea for this dish from Simon Yung, one of my Chinese chefs, who normally cooks sticky rice wrapped in a lotus leaf. The method has, in fact, come to be one of my favourite ways to cook fish: the aromatic and unique flavour of the lotus leaf and sesame oil combined with the other ingredients gives a dish with a special twist.

Incidentally, dried lotus leaves are available from any Chinese supermarket. Before using, simply soak in cold water, then rinse thoroughly to avoid any bitterness.

Lotus Leaves

Cover the lotus leaves with cold water and leave to soak for at least 3–4 hours or, preferably, overnight.

Drain the lotus leaves and rinse thoroughly under cold running water. Shake and squeeze each leaf gently to remove any excess water.

Salmon

Heat the sesame oil in a non-stick pan. Season the salmon with salt and pepper, then brown quickly on both sides and remove from the pan.

Using the same pan, sweat the shallots, peppers and garlic without colouring for 3 minutes. Add the mushrooms and stir-fry for a further 30 seconds. Season with salt and pepper. Remove from the pan and divide into 4 equal portions.

Place one lotus leaf in front of you and fold it in half crosswise. Place one-quarter of the vegetable mixture in the centre of the leaf, then place the salmon on top. Place another quarter of the vegetable mixture on top of the salmon. Finally, fold the leaf together like a parcel. Repeat this process with the other leaf and the remaining salmon and vegetables.

Place the parcels on a baking sheet and bake in the preheated oven for 10–15 minutes, depending upon the thickness of the salmon.

To Finish

Arrange the parcels on a serving dish. Just before placing on the table, cut them open with scissors and sprinkle with the finely chopped mixed herbs. The aroma that escapes will make your mouth water!

Red Mullet Escabeche with Samphire

(approximately 460 calories per portion)

This bright and colourful dish is best served slightly warm. The mullet is pan-fried and then marinated warm in a dressing of peppers and samphire, also known as glasswort, a type of seaweed. This can only be eaten when young, between April and July, and, unfortunately, it is not readily available. However, any reputable fishmonger should be able to order it for you or, alternatively, you can buy it in bottles from speciality shops. If you cannot get it, substitute very thin spears of asparagus.

Dressing
Mix all the ingredients together. (I find the easiest way to do this is to put everything into a small bottle, screw the lid on tightly and then give it a good shake.)

Fish
Heat the vegetable and sesame oils in a non-stick pan. Pat dry the fillets of mullet with a paper towel and season with salt and freshly ground pepper, then brown quickly in the pan, skin side first. Remove from the pan to a serving dish.

Using the same pan, sweat the red and yellow peppers and samphire for about 1 minute without colouring. Add the prepared dressing and simmer for a further minute. Adjust the seasoning if necessary. (If the samphire is bottled, do not add it until the dish is ready to serve.)

Pour the hot mixture over the fish and marinate for 10 minutes in a warm place. Baste with the liquid a few times.

To Finish
Serve in the same dish, or arrange on a plate, and garnish with fresh dill and rocket.

Serves 2

1 tbsp vegetable oil
1 tbsp sesame oil
4 red mullet fillets
Dressing
1 tbsp sesame oil
1 tbsp vegetable oil
2 tbsp fish stock or vegetable stock (see basic recipe, page 193)
1 tbsp white wine vinegar
salt and fresh ground pepper
Vegetables
½ red sweet pepper, seeds removed, cut into strips
½ yellow sweet pepper, seeds removed, cut into strips
50 g/2 oz fresh (or bottled) samphire (salicornia)
Garnish
fresh dill
rocket leaves (arugula) (optional)

Potted Salmon and Crab

(Approximately 250 calories per portion)

A very easy yet eye-catching first course that I developed for one of our annual polo events. Serve with toasted brown bread or melba toast.

Combine the crab meat, diced smoked salmon, shallots and dill in a bowl. Whisk together the vinegar and sesame oil and add to the salmon mixture. Season with salt, pepper and turmeric.

Place the 2 metal rings on a small flat tray. Divide the fish mixture in half and spoon into the metal rings. Spread the crème fraîche in equal quantities on top and smooth the surface. Refrigerate for at least 30 minutes or overnight.

To Finish
Arrange the cucumber slices in the centre of the plates to form a ring. Remove the metal rings from around the potted salmon and crab, then carefully lift them and place in the centre of the cucumber ring. To add a finishing touch, garnish with dill and a teaspoon of salmon roe.

Note: Instead of using metal rings, you can put the mixture into ramekin dishes and spread the crème fraîche on top. Garnish and serve in the ramekins.

Serves 2

75 g/3 oz white crab meat
75 g/3 oz smoked salmon, diced
25 g/1 oz (2 tbsp) peeled shallots, and finely chopped
¼ tsp chopped fresh dill
1 tsp white wine vinegar
2 tsp sesame oil
salt and freshly ground pepper
1 pinch of turmeric
75 ml/3 fl oz crème fraîche
Garnish
½ cucumber (English hothouse cucumber), cut into 3 mm/⅛ inch slices
2 sprigs of dill (optional)
salmon roe (optional)
You will need
2 metal rings, each 7 cm/3 inches in diameter

A WORLD OF FLAVOURS

SESAME OIL

Fillet of Sea Bass with Chinese Greens and Bacon (page 112)

Fillet of Sea Bass with Chinese Greens and Bacon

Serves 2

- 75 g/3 oz unsmoked streaky bacon rashers (thick bacon slices), rind removed, cut across into small finger-thick strips
- 4 tsp sesame oil
- ½ tsp chopped fresh coriander (cilantro)
- 1 pinch of finely grated lemon
- 2 thick sea bass fillets, each about 150 g/5 oz
- 6 new potatoes, peeled and part-cooked ready for roasting (see basic recipe, page 194)
- 6 medium-sized shiitake mushrooms, cut in half
- 6 pieces of Chinese flowering cabbage, leaves removed, stalks cooked and refreshed
- 2 bay leaves, deep-fried, to garnish

Sauce

- 1 shallot, peeled and finely sliced
- 100 ml/4 fl oz red wine
- 2 tbsp port wine
- 100 ml/4 fl oz fish stock (see basic recipe, page 190)
- 2 tbsp double cream (heavy cream)
- 40 g/1 ½ oz (3 tbsp) butter, cut into cubes
- salt and freshly ground pepper

Oven temperature

180°C/350°F/Gas mark 4

(Approximately 710 calories per portion)

A personal favourite in which Eastern and Western flavours unite to transform fillets of sea bass.

Sauce

Combine the shallot, red wine, port wine and fish stock in a saucepan. Bring to the boil and simmer until only 3 tablespoons of liquid remain. Add the cream and return to the boil. Pass through a sieve into a smaller saucepan, pressing out all the liquid. Return to the boil and remove from the heat. Very slowly whisk the butter cubes into the sauce. Season to taste. Keep the sauce warm, but do not reheat or it will split.

Fish

Blanch the bacon strips in boiling water for a few seconds, drain and allow to cool. Mix 1 tsp of sesame oil with the chopped coriander and lemon zest and keep aside. Pierce the skin of the fillets with two fine cuts to prevent them from curling up when cooked.

Now what you are going to do is to form a pocket in each piece of fish into which you will put the coriander mixture. To do this, put one piece in front of you, skin side down. With a sharp knife cut a slit along the edge on one side, about halfway between the skin and top surface. Cut in gently, leaving about 5 mm/¼ inch intact along the other 3 sides. Repeat the process with the other piece of fish. Brush inside the pocket with the sesame and coriander mixture. Keep aside.

Heat a non-stick pan (choose one with an ovenproof handle) and add the remaining sesame oil. Add the bacon strips and brown them a little. Season the sea bass with salt and freshly ground pepper. Move the bacon strips to the side of the pan and put in the sea bass, skin side down. Brown, then turn the pieces over and transfer to the preheated oven. Bake for about 8 minutes or until cooked. Remove the fish and bacon from the pan and keep warm.

Add the potatoes to the pan, return to the oven and cook for 3–4 minutes. Add the mushrooms. When the mushrooms are cooked, add the Chinese cabbage stalks to the pan to warm through. Season with salt and freshly ground pepper.

To Finish

Place the sea bass in the centre of the plates and arrange the bacon strips, roast potatoes, mushrooms and Chinese cabbage stalks alternately around the fish. Place a deep-fried bay leaf vertically in the centre of the fish. Serve the sauce separately.

Chicken Kebabs

(Approximately 465 calories per skewer)

Here, marinated chicken kebabs are accompanied by a sweet pepper and yoghurt sauce. For the fullest flavour, barbecue the kebabs.

Chicken
Mix together all the ingredients for the marinade in a bowl. Cut the chicken into 3 cm/1 ¼ inch cubes and add them to the marinade. Mix well to coat. Cover and leave overnight in the refrigerator.

The next day, heat a non-stick pan, add the chicken cubes and cook for approximately 2 minutes or until golden brown. Remove from the pan, place on paper towels and keep aside.

Sauce
Heat the sesame oil in a saucepan. Add the shallot, garlic and red pepper and sweat for 2 minutes without colouring. Add the white wine and chicken stock and bring to the boil. Reduce the heat, cover with a lid and simmer until the pepper is completely cooked. Purée the mixture and pass through a fine sieve into a clean saucepan. Add the chopped tomato and bring back to the boil. Season with salt and freshly ground pepper and remove from the heat. Add the yoghurt, pine nuts and basil. Keep aside.

Vegetables
Cut the red pepper into 3 cm/1 ¼ inch square shapes. Cut the onion into similar pieces. Drop into boiling salted water and blanch for 2 minutes, ensuring that they remain crisp. Remove and refresh in a bowl of iced water. Drain and dry on paper towels.

Dressing the skewers
Thread a piece of chicken on to a skewer, followed by a piece of onion and a piece of pepper. Continue until all the chicken and vegetables are used up. Make sure they are not pressed too tightly against each other. Keep to one side until required.

To Finish
Season the kebabs and brush with oil, then place on a baking tray and grill for 5–6 minutes or until medium cooked. Alternatively, if the sun is shining, cook the kebabs on the barbecue for 6–8 minutes. Serve the sauce, at room temperature, separately.

Serves 2

2 skinless boneless chicken breasts (breast halves)
1 small red sweet pepper, seeds removed
½ onion, peeled
salt and freshly ground pepper
1 tbsp vegetable oil

Marinade

½ lemon, juiced
2 tbsp sesame oil
½ garlic clove, peeled and finely chopped
1 pinch of finely grated fresh ginger

Sauce

1 tbsp sesame oil
1 shallot, peeled and finely chopped
1 garlic clove, peeled and finely chopped
1 red sweet pepper, seeds removed, cut into 1 cm/½ inch cubes
50 ml/2 fl oz white wine
100 ml/4 fl oz chicken stock (see basic recipe, page 190)
1 medium-sized tomato, peeled, seeded and coarsely chopped
2 tbsp plain yoghurt
2 tbsp toasted pine nuts, coarsely chopped
1 tsp finely chopped fresh basil

You will need

2 skewers (If wooden, cover them with cold water and soak for about 10 minutes before using, to prevent them from burning.)

Grill (broiler)
medium hot

Serves 2

2 skinless chicken breasts (breast halves)
2 tbsp white breadcrumbs
2 tbsp sesame seeds
1 egg
salt and freshly ground pepper
2 tbsp flour
2 tbsp sesame oil
1 tsp butter
1 lime, sliced, to garnish

Marinade
1 lime, juiced
1 tsp light soy sauce
½ tsp finely chopped fresh coriander (cilantro)

Oven temperature
200°C/400°F/Gas mark 6

Roasted sesame chicken

(Approximately 260 calories per portion)

A simple yet tasty way with chicken that combines both sesame seeds and sesame oil.

Marinade

Mix together all the ingredients for the marinade. Place the chicken breasts in the marinade and refrigerate for at least 10 minutes.

Chicken

Mix the breadcrumbs and sesame seeds together on a small tray. Beat the egg lightly in a medium-sized bowl. Place the tray and bowl in front of you.

Remove the chicken breasts from the marinade and pat dry on paper towels. Season with salt and freshly ground pepper and dust thoroughly with flour, pressing it on lightly with your hands. Now dip the breasts into the egg wash, making sure that each breast is completely coated. Shake off any excess egg, then place in the tray of breadcrumbs and sesame seeds. Cover the breasts completely with the mixture, pressing it on lightly with your hands. Shake gently to remove any excess.

To Finish

Heat a roasting tray in the preheated oven and add the oil and butter. Place the chicken breasts in the tray and bake in the middle of the oven for about 15 minutes, basting frequently, until cooked and golden brown in colour. Garnish with a slice of lime, and serve.

Limes

The most widely available lime in the west is round (or a rounded oval), about the size of an egg, with thin smooth skin. It is very juicy, with about two to three times more juice than a normal lemon. The juice can be used in jams and pickles, with sweets, fish or meat, or as a salad dressing. The coloured skin, or zest, can be finely chopped and added to fish dishes as well as to desserts. Or the lime can simply be used as a less tart substitute for lemon.

Flying from Switzerland to Bali, squeezed into my economy seat, felt like flying to the other end of the world – or rather it made me realise just how immense the planet is. During the long flight I had time to read my travel guide and make some notes in my travel-log about where to go and what to see.

I'd been told that the best way to see the sights was by motorcycle, so on arrival one of the first things I did was to find a motorcycle dealer. I was surprised to learn that I couldn't hire a bike without taking a test. So the next morning I presented myself at the police station in Denpaser. Happily, I had no trouble completing the questionnaire, with the help of the friendly police officers, and then I had to drive around the courtyard to their satisfaction. A photograph and fingerprint later, I had my licence and my motorcycle. I was at last free to discover the island!

After seeing some of the sights and breathtaking scenery, I headed up to Lake Batur. The road became steeper and steeper, and I really wasn't sure if my bike would make it – or perhaps it was my driving skill! But eventually I reached the top of the pass and was rewarded with an unforgettable view. It was like being in a theatre just as the show begins: the curtain of mist lifted to reveal a dark blue lake flanked by massive volcano peaks.

The following day, wanting to walk on top of the crater, I hired a local guide to lead me there. When we started out, the weather was overcast and dull – ideal for walking – but after climbing for about 1 $1/2$ hours the clouds suddenly dispersed and within minutes it was as hot as a furnace. Unfortunately, there still proved to be another hour to go before we reached the top. It was very difficult to walk on the loose gravel of the volcano, and by then my legs were aching and my heels were covered in blisters. But in the end, the view and the experience made it all worthwhile.

On returning to the camp, I bought some water and, as was suggested to me, added a squeeze of lime. It was like a tonic – especially as it was followed by a most welcome and relaxing bath in the hot springs. I felt like a king lying in my warm pool under the evening stars.

The lime I used was completely different to any I had seen before. It was shaped more like a pear, with a very wrinkly skin and flesh that was pale green in colour. The taste was quite sour and bitter. I was told it was a caffir or kaffir lime, mainly used for cooking but also in a number of Balinese medicines. The juice is even used for washing hair.

This adventure made me want to learn more about limes, so on my return home I went to the library and did some reading. The information I found was quite confusing because there are about 900 different species of lime, the majority of which are grown in the Tropics. Citrus fruits seem to have originated in East Asia, and are probably the result of 10 or more species being crossed, selected and re-crossed. This has happened so many times that even traders and experts disagree over the origins of the different fruits.

A few years ago, I went back to Bali to organise a culinary exchange visit. To ensure that we had all the correct ingredients for the visiting chefs, I went with Chef Marcel Isaak and one of the locals, Chef Kefut Mardang, to the buzzing morning market. There had been rain in some parts of the island over the previous few days, and as a result there was an almost overwhelming variety of produce in the market. This time I found yet another new lime, which was about the size of a walnut, with a smooth skin and sweet-tart juice. It seemed to me that my discoveries about limes would never end!

A *World of Flavours*

LIMES

Santen Seafood Salad

Serves 4

1 small new carrot, scrubbed
4 baby sweetcorn
25 g/1 oz shelled fresh broad beans (2 tbsp fava beans)
100 g/4 oz sole fillet, skin removed
100 g/4 oz salmon fillet, skin removed
4 raw king prawns (large shrimp), peeled and deveined
500 ml/16 fl oz fish stock (see basic recipe, page 190)
1 small tomato, peeled, seeded and cut into 3 mm/1/8 inch cubes
25 g/1 oz oakleaf lettuce
25 g/1 oz curly endivee (frisée)
a few sprigs of dill, to garnish

Dressing

2 limes, juiced
4 tbsp sunflower oil
1 tbsp canned unsweetened coconut cream
1/4 tsp each chopped fresh chervil, parsley and chives
salt and freshly ground pepper

(Approximately 240 calories per portion)

The salad is based on a dish I first ate whilst I was living in a small guest house in Jakarta. Santen translated literally means coconut milk, although, in this recipe I use coconut 'cream'. This is available from some supermarkets, notably those offering Eastern goods. However, coconut milk is now easily obtainable and if you leave this to stand in the refrigerator, the thick white liquid that gathers at the surface can happily be used as coconut 'cream'. Incidently, coconut milk or cream must be used whilst fresh (it keeps for about 2 days once opened), but unfortunately it does not freeze well.

Vegetables

Bring a pan of salted water to the boil. Add the carrot and cook until tender but still crisp. Refresh immediately by plunging into a bowl of iced water, then drain and cut into 3 mm/1/8 inch slices. Repeat the process with the sweetcorn, using the same water. Repeat again with the broad beans, but peel them and leave them whole. Retain 2 tbsp of the cooking water for the dressing and discard the rest.

Dressing

Strain the lime juice into a bowl and mix in the reserved vegetable cooking water. Add the sunflower oil and coconut cream. Use a handblender to mix (or mix the dressing in a blender). Finally, add the chopped herbs and season with salt and freshly ground pepper.

Fish

Cut the sole into 4 equal pieces. Do the same with the salmon. Season all the fish and the prawns with salt and pepper.

Bring the fish stock to the boil and add the sole, salmon and prawns. Simmer gently for about 1 minute, then remove from the heat and leave for 5 minutes. Remove the fish from the hot stock with a slotted spoon and place on a small tray. Immediately spoon over half of the dressing and marinate for about 15 minutes.

To Finish

Mix together the vegetables and tomato and marinate in the remaining dressing. Meanwhile, arrange the endive and lettuce leaves on the plates in a ring. Drain the marinated vegetables and place in the centre. Place the fish and prawns on the vegetables and garnish with dill. Use the marinade from the vegetables as a vinaigrette for the salad leaves.

Deep-fried Vegetables with a Guacamole Dip

(Approximately 720 calories per portion)

This recipe takes time, but the combination of the warm crunchy vegetables dipped in the smooth guacamole is sensational. It can be served either as a snack with drinks or plated individually for a first course. The vegetables, the batter and the dip can be prepared before your guests come, but the deep frying must be done just before serving.

Vegetables

Trim the broccoli and cauliflower florets to remove the end parts of the stem. Cut the courgettes and aubergine into small finger-sized pieces. Put the vegetables aside until required.

Guacamole dip

The easiest way to make this is using a food processor; however, if you don't have one you can mix with a fork. Peel the avocados and remove the stone. Place the flesh in the bowl of a food processor and add the garlic, lime juice, yoghurt and vegetable stock. Blend to make a smooth purée, then add the olive oil. Season with pepper, salt and chilli powder to taste. Finally, stir in the chopped tomato and coriander. Scoop into a small glass bowl, cover closely and keep in the refrigerator until required.

Batter

Mix the flour with the oil, then add the white wine and continue mixing until all the lumps disappear. Whisk the egg white until stiff and fold it gently but thoroughly into the mixture. Season with salt and freshly ground white pepper.

To Finish

Just before serving, cook the vegetables. Heat the oil in a deep fat fryer or saucepan to about 180°C/350°F. Season the vegetables with salt and freshly ground white pepper, then dust with flour. Dip into the batter and drop into the hot oil. Deep-fry until golden brown, then remove and drain on paper towels. Keep warm until all the pieces of vegetable are fried. Arrange all the vegetables on a plate and serve with the guacamole dip.

Serves 4

175 g/6 oz (1 3/4 cups) small broccoli florets
175 g/6 oz small cauliflower florets
175 g/6 oz courgettes (zucchini)
175 g/6 oz aubergine (eggplant)
corn oil to deep fry the vegetables
flour to coat the vegetables
salt and freshly ground white pepper

Guacamole dip

2 ripe avocados
1 garlic clove, peeled and crushed with a knife or garlic press
1 lime, juiced and strained
1 tsp plain yoghurt
50 ml/2 fl oz vegetable stock (see basic recipe, page 193)
1 tbsp olive oil
chilli powder to taste
small tomato, peeled, seeded and finely chopped
1 tbsp chopped fresh coriander (cilantro)

Batter

175 g/6 oz plain flour (1 1/4 cups all-purpose flour)
3 tbsp olive oil
300 ml/10 fl oz white wine
1 egg white

A WORLD OF FLAVOURS

*Lime-flavoured
Chicken and
Noodle Soup
(page 124)*

Lime-flavoured chicken and noodle soup

Serves 4

1.2 lt/ 2 pt (5 cups) chicken stock (see basic recipe, page 190)
1 piece of lemon grass, 5 cm/2 inches long, outer leaves removed
1 tsp ground cardamom
½ bay leaf
4 chicken drumsticks
1 tbsp sesame oil
¼ onion, peeled and finely chopped
½ small white of leek, cut into small dice
1 small new carrot, cut into small cubes
25 g/1 oz fine Chinese egg noodles, cut in half
1 tbsp light soy sauce
½ lime, juiced
salt and freshly ground pepper
fresh coriander leaves (cilantro), to garnish

(Approximately 160 calories per portion)

Soups were always a welcome and inexpensive meal during my early years of travelling. Often I would close my eyes and not look too closely at the ingredients! But when I make this and close my eyes, the aroma brings back many happy memories.

Put the chicken stock in a large pot and add the lemon grass, cardamom and bay leaf. Bring slowly to the boil, then add the chicken drumsticks and simmer for about 30 minutes.

Take the drumsticks from the stock and remove the skin and bones. Cut the meat into small dice and keep aside. Strain the stock through a fine sieve and reserve.

Heat the sesame oil in a small saucepan and sweat the onion, leek and carrot for about 1 minute over a low heat. Add the strained stock and bring to the boil. Add the noodles, then remove from the heat, cover with a lid and leave for 4 minutes or until the noodles are cooked but still 'al dente'. Add the soy sauce and lime juice. Season with pepper, plus a very little salt if necessary – remember to taste first as the soy sauce is salty. Finally, add the diced chicken meat.

To Finish

If necessary, reheat gently – do not boil. Ladle into 4 warm bowls, garnish with coriander leaves and serve.

Chilled crab and cucumber soup

Serve 4

2 large cucumbers (English hothouse cucumbers)
1 tomato
1 tsp caster sugar (granulated sugar)
1 tsp salt
1 lime, juiced
250 ml/8 fl oz single cream (light cream)
1 tsp finely chopped fresh dill
100 g/4 oz white crab meat
cayenne pepper
salt and freshly ground pepper

(Approximately 180 calories per portion)

Serve this soup well chilled on a warm summer's day.

Vegetables

Peel the cucumbers, then cut them in half lengthwise. Using a teaspoon, scoop out the seeds and discard. Chop the flesh coarsely and place in a bowl.

Next, peel the tomato. To make light work of this, first plunge the tomato into a pan of boiling water for 20 seconds, then immediately into a bowl of iced water to cool. The skin will then slide off quite easily. Cut the tomato into quarters, remove the seeds and chop the flesh coarsely. Place in the bowl with the cucumber.

Sprinkle the sugar, salt and lime juice over the cucumber and tomato and toss gently together. Allow to stand for about 30 minutes.

Soup

Drain the cucumber and tomato mixture, discarding any liquid, then purée in a blender or food processor. Add the cream and blend again for about 10 seconds. Pass the purée through a fine sieve into a bowl.

Add the chopped dill and crab meat. Season with cayenne pepper, salt and freshly ground pepper. Refrigerate until very cold.

To Finish

Divide the soup among 4 chilled bowls and serve immediately.

Fillets of Sole with Roasted Peppers

(Approximately 110 calories per portion)

Serve this light, warm first course with slices of toasted Italian or French bread to lap up the delicious dressing. Note how easily the skins are removed from the peppers for this recipe – I learnt this method very recently from Gilly King, who in turn learnt it from her mother.

Peppers
Place the whole peppers on a baking tray and roast in the preheated oven for about 15 minutes. They will retain their colour, but brown slightly. Remove them from the oven and put them in a plastic bag. Tie loosely and leave to cool. Then open the bag and simply peel the skin off. (Do this over a bowl so you can catch all the pepper juice.) Cut each pepper into quarters and remove the seeds. Keep aside. Reserve the juice from the bowl and plastic bag.

Sauce
Heat the oil in a saucepan and sweat the shallot until translucent, without colouring. Add the capers, vegetable stock, lime juice and reserved pepper juice. Season to taste with salt and freshly ground pepper. Return to the boil, then remove from the heat and add the parsley. Keep aside.

Fish
Heat the oil in a non-stick pan. Season the sole fillets with salt and pepper and cut each in half. Dust with flour, pat it on and then shake off any excess flour. Fry until golden brown on each side and cooked. Remove from the pan, put on to paper towel and keep warm.

To Finish
Return the sauce to the boil. Arrange the peppers on 4 plates and pour the hot sauce over. Arrange the sole fillets on top of the peppers and serve.

Serves 4

3 medium-sized sweet peppers, any colour
2 tbsp vegetable oil
4 sole fillets, each about 75 g/3 oz
salt and freshly ground pepper
flour to dust the fillets

Sauce

4 tbsp vegetable oil
1 shallot, peeled and finely chopped
2 tbsp capers, drained and roughly chopped
4 tbsp vegetable stock (see basic recipe, page 193)
1 lime, juiced
2 tsp finely chopped parsley

Oven temperature
240°C/475°F/Gas mark 9

Grilled Tuna Steak with a Virgin Olive Oil and Garlic Sauce

Serves 4

4 tuna steaks, each about 100 g/4 oz
salt and freshly ground pepper
oil to brush steaks

Sauce

1 thick slice of white bread, crust removed
1 garlic clove, peeled and crushed with a knife or garlic press
5 egg yolks
1 pinch of English mustard powder
50 ml/2 fl oz virgin olive oil
250 ml/8 fl oz sunflower oil
½ lime, juiced
100 ml/4 fl oz fish stock (see basic recipe, page 190) at room temperature
1 tsp chopped fresh dill
1 tbsp chopped fresh basil

Grill (broiler)
very hot

(Approximately 820 calories per portion)

As a young chef I worked alongside Giuseppe, a true Italian, who was full of passion for food. It was he who introduced me to virgin olive oil, with its distinguished, subtle flavour and purity, with just a hint of acidity. I will never forget the day I tried to use it to pan-fry a steak. Giuseppe saw what I was doing and his Italian temper flared! Shouting at me, he made it very clear that this type of oil was not to be used for frying!

I certainly learnt from this mistake that virgin olive oil is best used for dressings only, and it is for this reason that it is a clear favourite for this particular recipe.

Sauce

Dip the bread in cold water and soak for a few seconds; do not leave it too long or it will become mushy. Then remove it from the water and gently squeeze out any excess. Place in the bowl of a food processor.

Add the garlic, egg yolks and mustard. Blend to a 'sticky' paste. Then, with the machine still running, slowly drizzle in the oils until all has been absorbed and you have a thickish emulsion. Add the lime juice and fish stock. Blend for a few more seconds to mix, then taste and season with salt and freshly ground pepper. Stir in the chopped dill and basil and pour into a serving dish.

To Finish

Season the tuna steaks and brush with oil. Grill, turning once, until cooked. Serve with the sauce handed separately.

Lime-Crusted Fillet of Brill

(Approximately 500 calories per portion)

Here I use finely chopped lime and orange zest to flavour the crust for the brill.

Crust
Combine all the ingredients in a food processor. Blend together quickly, and keep aside.

Sauce
Melt the butter in a non-stick pan and sweat the shallot until translucent, without colouring. Add the white wine, bring to the boil and simmer to reduce to half the quantity. Then add the fish stock, return to the boil and simmer to reduce to half the quantity again. Now add the cream and reduce to a coating consistency. Season with salt and pepper and strain through a sieve into a clean pan. Reheat before serving.

Fish
About 10 minutes before eating, cook the fish. Season the brill fillets with salt and freshly ground white pepper. Brush each with mustard. Spread the crust mixture equally over the 4 fish fillets.

Butter an ovenproof dish and place the fish in it, crust side up. Bake in the middle of the preheated oven for about 8 minutes. The fish should be cooked and the crust golden brown. If it isn't sufficiently coloured, pop it under the grill quickly. Serve immediately with the hot sauce.

Serves 4

- 4 brill fillets, each 175–200 g/6–7 oz
- salt and freshly ground white pepper
- 1 tbsp whole-grain French mustard
- 25 g/1 oz (2 tbsp) butter

Crust
- ¼ tsp finely chopped orange zest
- ¼ tsp finely chopped lime zest
- ½ tsp each chopped fresh dill, parsley and basil
- 50 g/2 oz (1 cup) white breadcrumbs (from 3 slices of bread)
- 25 g/1 oz (2 tbsp) soft unsalted butter

Sauce
- 25 g/1 oz (2 tbsp) unsalted butter
- 1 shallot, peeled and sliced
- 50 ml/2 fl oz dry white wine
- 100 ml/4 fl oz fish stock (see basic recipe, page 190)
- 150 ml/5 fl oz double cream (heavy cream)

Oven temperature
200°C/400°F/Gas mark 6

Smoked Mackerel Gratin

(Approximately 365 calories per portion)

Try this topped with a sharp creamy glaze and serve with mashed potatoes and salad.

Sauce
Remove a thin layer of skin or zest from the lime half. Chop enough zest very finely to fill ½ tsp, and keep aside.

Now extract the juice from the lime half and pour it into a saucepan. Add the shallot and fish stock and bring to the boil. Simmer gently to reduce to half the quantity. Add the cream and simmer for a further 3 minutes over medium heat. Strain the mixture through a sieve into a bowl and keep aside.

Mackerel
About 10 minutes before eating, place the mackerel fillets on an oven tray, skin side down, and heat in the preheated oven for about 5 minutes or until hot.

Glaze
Whilst the mackerel are warming, mix the egg yolk into the sauce. Add the mustard, spring onion, whipped cream and the finely chopped lime zest. Season with salt and freshly ground pepper.

To Finish
When the mackerel are hot, transfer them to a flameproof serving dish. Pour the glaze over them so that they are completely covered. Place under the preheated grill (broiler) and glaze until golden brown. Serve.

Serves 4

- 4 smoked mackerel fillets

Sauce
- ½ lime
- ½ shallot, peeled and finely chopped
- 100 ml/4 fl oz fish stock (see basic recipe, page 190)
- 100 ml/4 fl oz single cream (light cream)

Glaze
- 1 egg yolk
- 1 pinch of English mustard powder
- 1 spring onion (green onion), finely chopped
- 2 tbsp whipping cream (heavy cream), lightly whipped
- salt and freshly ground pepper

Oven temperature
180°C/350°F/Gas mark 4

Grill (broiler)
very hot

Lamb Chops with Limed Apricot Confit

(Approximately 470 calories per portion)

The sweetness of apricots and the sharpness of lime complement tender lamb chops to perfection.

Serves 2

- 1 tbsp vegetable oil
- 4 lamb cutlets (lamb rib chops), each about 75 g/3 oz, well trimmed
- salt and freshly ground pepper

Confit
- 2 shallots, peeled and finely chopped
- 2 dried apricots, coarsely chopped
- 2 tbsp sherry vinegar
- 1 lime, juiced
- 50 ml/2 fl oz lamb stock (see basic recipe, page 192)
- 1 tsp apricot jam
- 100 ml/4 fl oz double cream (heavy cream)

Oven temperature
180°C/350°F/Gas mark 4

Lamb Chops
Heat the vegetable oil in a non-stick pan. Season the chops with salt and freshly ground pepper and add them to the hot pan. Seal them quickly on both sides, then remove from the pan and place on a heated oven tray. Cook in the preheated oven for about 8 minutes, depending on size. They should still be pink and juicy inside. Remove the chops from the oven and keep them in a warm place.

Confit
Whilst the chops are in the oven, start preparing the confit. Use the same pan and the oil remaining from cooking the chops. Add the shallots and sweat over medium heat until translucent and soft, without colouring (about 10 minutes).

Add the chopped apricots, sherry vinegar and lime juice and bring to the boil. Simmer over medium heat, stirring constantly, until no liquid is left.

Add the lamb stock, apricot jam and cream, and simmer for a further minute. Season with salt and pepper. Then pass as much as you can through a sieve, pressing lightly with a spoon, into a saucepan. Keep both the confit in the sieve and the sauce.

To Finish
Place the lamb chops on 2 plates. Divide the apricot confit left in the sieve on top of each chop. Bring the sauce in the pan to the boil and serve separately.

Medallions of Pork in Lime Sauce

(Approximately 365 calories per portion)

Here I use medallions of pork which are cut from the fillet or tenderloin, but these could easily be replaced by pork steaks or chops to make the dish more economical.

Garnish
Mix the lime zest with the parsley and garlic. Keep aside.

Marinade
Mix together all the ingredients for the marinade, then pour over the meat and allow it to marinate for at least 20 minutes or overnight.

Remove the meat from the marinade and pat dry with paper towels. Reserve the marinade. Heat the oil in a frying pan. Season the medallions with salt and pepper and fry until golden brown on both sides. Remove from the pan (keep it aside) and place the medallions on a baking tray. Cook in the preheated oven for 6–8 minutes (medium/well), depending on the thickness of the meat.

Sauce
In the meantime, prepare the sauce. Using the same frying pan, add the marinade and the veal stock. Bring to the boil and simmer over low heat for 3 minutes. Add the cream and simmer for a further minute, then season with salt and freshly ground pepper. Keep aside.

To Finish
Remove the medallions from the baking tray and place on a serving dish. Bring the sauce to the boil again and pour over the meat. Sprinkle with the lime/parsley garnish and serve.

Serves 4

8 medallions of pork, each 50 g/2 oz
2 tbsp vegetable oil
salt and freshly ground pepper

Garnish

½ tsp grated lime zest
1 tbsp chopped parsley
½ garlic clove, peeled and finely chopped

Marinade

1 tbsp vegetable oil
1 garlic clove, peeled and crushed with a knife or garlic press
1 tsp lime juice
freshly ground pepper
1 tsp English mustard powder

Sauce

100 ml/4 fl oz brown veal stock (see basic recipe, page 191)
150 ml/5 fl oz double cream (heavy cream)

Oven temperature

180°C/350°F/Gas mark 4

Medallions of Pork in Lime Sauce (page 129)

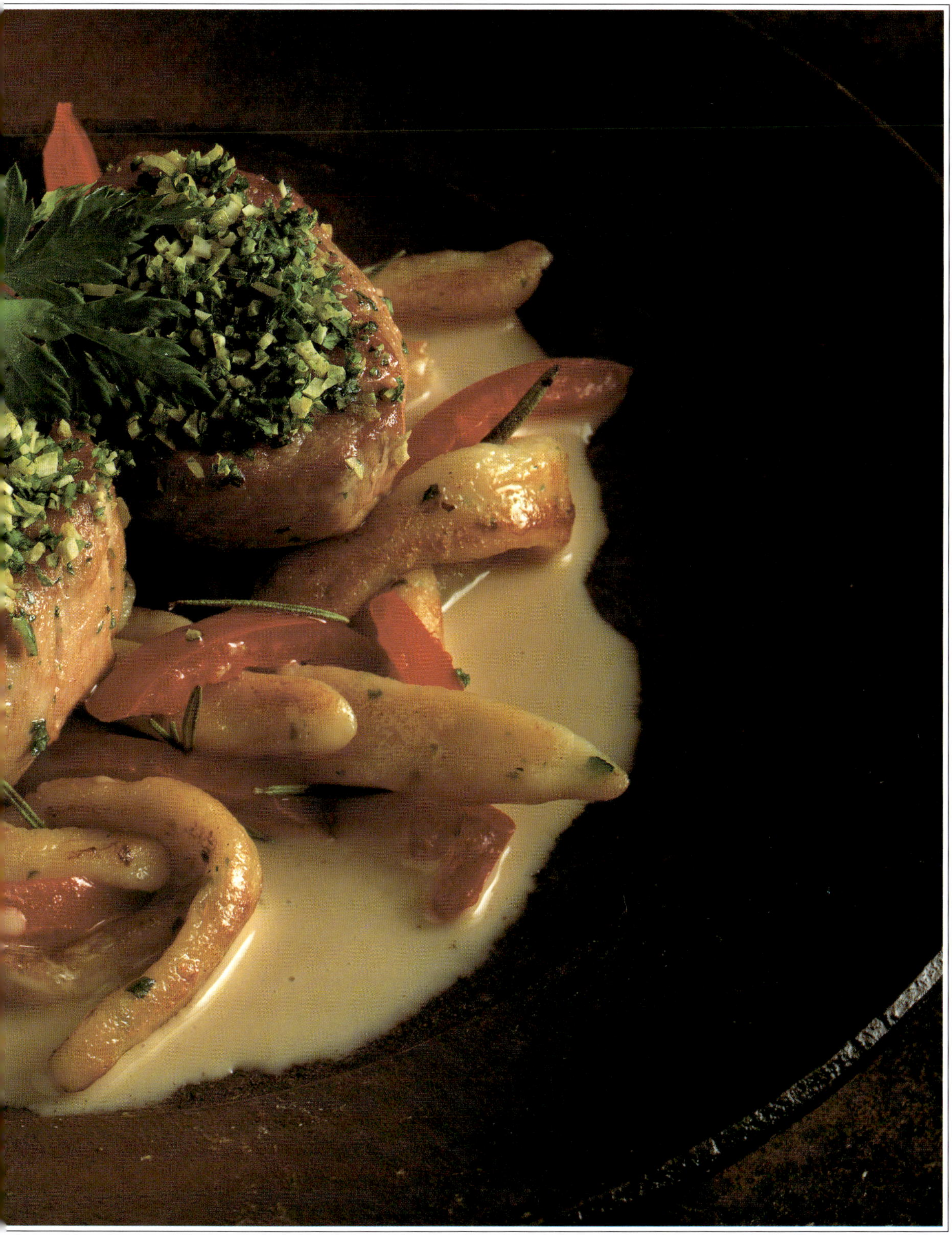

Mackerel with Peri-Peri Sauce

SERVES 4

4 medium-sized mackerel fillets, each about 100 g/4 oz
1 tbsp vegetable oil

Peri-peri sauce

50 ml/2 fl oz vegetable oil
½ shallot, peeled and finely chopped
1 garlic clove, peeled and crushed with a knife or garlic press
2 pinches of finely chopped fresh hot chilli pepper (seeded)
1 green sweet pepper, seeds removed, cut into 1 cm/½ inch cubes
8 medium-sized tomatoes, peeled and coarsely chopped
1 lime, juiced
salt and freshly ground pepper
1 tbsp chopped parsley
½ tbsp chopped fresh basil

(Approximately 390 calories per portion)

I first tasted 'peri-peri' at one of the many delicious meals I've eaten at the home of my parents-in-law. They, in turn, originally enjoyed it with fish, seafood or chicken in the then Portuguese colony of Mozambique. I've adapted the recipe so that here its fiery sharpness complements the oily flesh of fresh mackerel.

Peri-peri sauce
Heat the vegetable oil in saucepan and sweat the shallot and garlic over medium heat until translucent, without colouring. Add the chilli and sweet pepper and sweat for a further minute. Then add the tomatoes and simmer for 15 minutes. Finally, add the lime juice and season with salt and pepper. Keep aside until required.

Mackerel
Season the fillets with salt and freshly ground white pepper. Use a sharp knife to make one or two 1 cm/½ inch cuts through the skin down the centre of each fillet, to prevent it curling up when cooking.

Heat the oil in non-stick pan and fry the mackerel fillets, skin side first, until golden brown on both sides and cooked. They might still curl a little. Remove from the pan and place in a dish. Keep warm.

To Finish
Bring the sauce to the boil and add the parsley and basil. Spoon the sauce on to a serving dish, place the cooked mackerel on top and serve.

Baked Sea Bream with Asparagus in a Lime Sauce

SERVES 2

8 medium-sized green asparagus spears
2 tbsp vegetable oil
2 sea bream fillets (porgy), each 150 g/5 oz, scales removed
salt and freshly ground pepper
chopped fresh chervil and dill, to garnish

Sauce

1 tbsp vegetable oil
½ shallot, peeled and finely chopped
50 g/2 oz shiitake mushroom, cut into quarters
½ lime, juiced
100 ml/4 fl oz double cream (heavy cream)
1 pinch of grated lime zest

Oven temperature

200°C/400°F/Gas mark 6

(Approximately 561 calories per portion)

If you haven't tried sea bream before, this recipe is a must. Here the subtle flavour of this fish is enhanced by the addition of asparagus and shiitake mushrooms. Serve a little plain rice or boiled potatoes to enjoy with the sauce.

Asparagus
Snap or cut the woody ends off the asparagus spears and, if necessary, peel the stalks. Then cut each spear into 2.5 cm/1 inch pieces. Cook in a little boiling salted water until tender but still a little crisp. Remove from the cooking liquid using a slotted spoon, and refresh immediately in a bowl of iced water. Drain and keep aside. Reserve 100 ml/4 fl oz of the cooking liquid for the sauce.

Sea bream
Heat the vegetable oil in a non-stick pan. Season the sea bream with salt and freshly ground pepper and pan-fry over medium heat until golden brown on both sides. Remove from the pan and place on a baking tray. Bake in the preheated oven for 5–8 minutes (depending on the thickness of the fillet) until cooked.

SAUCE

Whilst the sea bream is in the oven, prepare the sauce. Using the same pan as used to seal the fish, heat the vegetable oil and sweat the shallot over medium heat until translucent, without colouring. Add the mushrooms, lime juice and reserved asparagus cooking liquid. Bring to the boil and simmer for 2-3 minutes over medium heat. Add the cream and return to the boil. Then add the asparagus pieces and lime zest. Return to the boil again and season with salt and pepper.

TO FINISH

Place the asparagus and mushroom mixture on a plate. Remove the fish from the oven and place on top. To add a finishing touch, garnish with the herbs and sauce.

LIME CHICKEN WITH MUSHROOMS

(Approximately 600 calories per portion)

Marinating is widely used in many different cuisines, either to tenderize or to enhance flavour. In this recipe, chicken breasts are marinated to give a unique flavour to the finished dish.

MARINADE

First, using a sharp knife or vegetable peeler, remove a thin layer of skin or zest from the lime half. Very finely chop enough zest to fill ½ tsp, and reserve for the sauce. Next juice the lime half and place in a dish large enough to hold the chicken breasts. Add all the other ingredients for the marinade and mix together. Turn the chicken breasts in the marinade to coat them, then marinate for about 30 minutes in a cool place.

Remove the chicken breasts from the marinade, reserving it for the sauce. Heat the oil in a non-stick pan and seal the breasts on both sides. Transfer them to an ovenproof dish and cook in the preheated oven for about 10 minutes.

SAUCE

Whilst the chicken breasts are in the oven, prepare the sauce. Using the same pan as before, melt the butter. Add the mushrooms and brown slightly. Then add the marinade, bring to the boil and boil for about 1 minute. Add the cream and boil until a creamy consistency is obtained. Add the reserved lime zest and season with salt and freshly ground pepper. Allow to cool slightly, then add the lightly beaten egg yolk.

TO FINISH

Remove the chicken breasts from the oven, pour over the sauce, place under the grill (broiler) and brown evenly. Serve immediately.

SERVES 2

2 skinless chicken breasts (breast halves), each about 180 g/6 oz

2 tbsp vegetable oil

Marinade

½ lime

salt and freshly ground white pepper

1 pinch of ground ginger

4 tsp dry sherry

1 pinch of English mustard powder

Sauce

25 g/1 oz (2 tbsp) butter

50 g/2 oz (¼ cup) button mushrooms, sliced

250 ml/8 fl oz single cream (light cream)

1 egg yolk, lightly beaten

Oven temperature

180°C/350°F/Gas mark 4

Grill (broiler)

very hot

A WORLD OF FLAVOURS

Peach and Mascarpone Mousse (page 136)

Peach and Mascarpone Mousse

Serves 4

8 ripe peaches, yellow or white

Syrup

750 ml/25 fl oz (3 cups) water

200 g/8 oz (1 cup) caster sugar (granulated sugar)

Mousse

¼ tsp very finely chopped lime zest

1 tbsp lime juice

¼ tsp pure vanilla essence (vanilla extract)

4 ½ tbsp caster sugar (granulated sugar)

2 tsp unflavoured gelatine powder

2 tbsp white rum

100 g/4 oz (½ cup) mascarpone cheese

100 ml/4 fl oz double cream (heavy cream), whipped

Garnish

fresh mint leaves

(Approximately 390 calories per portion)

To achieve the true flavour of this recipe wait until the height of summer, when peaches are at their peak. Combined with the mascarpone cheese it makes an unusual, rich and delicious dessert.

Peaches

Bring a pan of water to the boil then drop in the ripe peaches. After about 40 seconds, remove from the water using a slotted spoon and refresh immediately in a bowl of iced water. Peel and keep aside.

Syrup

Bring the water and sugar to the boil in the pan, add the peaches and simmer, covered, for 3 minutes. Remove from the heat and allow to cool, covered, in the liquid. Remove the peaches from the liquid, cut 2 of the peaches into 1cm/½ inch dice and keep aside in a bowl. Cut the remaining 6 peaches in half, remove the stones and keep aside.

Mousse

Add the lime zest, juice, vanilla essence and sugar to the diced peaches. Using a hand blender or food processor, purée and pour into a saucepan.

Heat on top of the stove, then remove from heat and sprinkle over the gelatine powder. Whisk it in together with the rum. Allow to cool. Mix in the mascarpone cheese and fold in the whipped cream. Finally, spoon the mixture into a bowl, and refrigerate for at least 4 hours or until set.

To Finish

Before serving, spoon the mixture into a piping bag and pipe in equal portions on top of each half peach. Arrange 3 half peaches per person on each plate, pour some of the syrup around. Garnish with mint and serve. Pour any remaining mousse into a bowl and serve separately.

Coriander

Coriander is, in fact, indigenous to the Mediterranean region, but is nowadays cultivated all over the world and so is readily obtainable. All parts of the plant are used: the leaves, stalks and roots as a popular herb (called cilantro in some parts of the world) and the seeds (which are really the dried ripe fruit) as a spice. The leaves and seeds each have quite a different aroma, taste and character.

A WORLD OF FLAVOURS

CORIANDER

Following a sensational trek in the Golden Triangle, up in the north of Thailand, I had the most wonderful experience. I shared a bath in a river with a herd of elephants! At first I was afraid to get into the water with the giants, but encouraged by their keeper, I rolled up my trouser legs and joined the elephants for their morning bath. What an experience! I even scrubbed their backs with a coconut shell! Only a photograph could prove my story back home.

Travelling back to Bangkok, I continued on to Ayutthaya, one of the ancient cities of Thailand, where I met an Australian who, like me, was on a voyage of discovery. From him I learnt of a fascinating trip by boat to a gypsy village on stilts, just a few hours outside the city. This, he told me, was a place not to be missed.

Determined to go there, I asked the concierge at my guesthouse to write in Thai the name of the ferry terminal I should start from, so that the tuk-tuk driver would know where to take me early the next morning. (Tuk tuks are the three-wheeled vehicles with motorcycle engines that take you round town very quickly – except when you are stuck in a traffic jam!) I thought it wise to have my destination written down as I had had communication problems before.

The following morning, I got up confidently at the crack of dawn, gave one of the tuk-tuk drivers my handwritten note and set off. After about half an hour I asked him if he knew where he was going. He replied, 'Okay, no problem.' After another 20 minutes or so, having passed the same buildings again, I began to worry. Finally, he stopped outside a rather modern building. I paid him the agreed fare and walked in the direction he had pointed. But after walking for a few minutes, I could see no sign of a ferry terminal or, in fact, of any water.

Feeling very angry and thwarted, I had to give up on my plans to visit the gypsy village, but what had started out disastrously became one of my lucky days. Wandering back to the guesthouse, I came upon one of the most spectacular open-air markets that I had ever visited, just in front of the Grand Palace.

The stalls were simply covered with sheets of colourful fabric or umbrellas, to protect the fragile goods from the burning tropical sun. And what goods there were. Imagine wild honey, still in the hive, next to washing powder. And every imaginable kind of fruit and vegetable (many of which I didn't recognise). Plus wild cats, monkeys, fried grasshoppers, and even a pig's head simmering in a pot on one of the open food stalls. Near this was a display of dried fish, shellfish and small shrimps piled high. The smell in the heat was overwhelming.

There was a gorgeous display of fresh herbs and exotic seasonings – again, many unfamiliar to me at the time: kaffir lime leaves, brown tamarind pods, pandanus leaves with their sweet grass-like fragrance, balsam leaves. Amongst these I spotted something familiar, and squeezing a leaf between my fingers I smelled the unmistakable perfume of coriander..

Coriander leaves, which can be either thin and feathery or broad and flat, have a pleasant lingering taste. They are used as a herb in many different ways: to flavour curries, soups, salsas, meat and fish; in salads; deep-fried; or as a fresh garnish. They are available both fresh and dried.

The spice – coriander seeds – is sold both whole and ground to a powder. It has a sweet woody aroma and mild, slightly burning taste. Coriander as a spice is used in both sweet and savoury dishes. It is one which I particularly like to use in my recipes. The essential oil is also used in both the pharmaceutical and perfumery industries.

Chicken and French bean salad

(Approximately 245 calories per portion)

In this recipe the lightly browned chicken pieces are simmered together with the dressing to combine their flavours. The salad should then be served warm with fresh bread – pitta pockets are my choice.

Serves 2

- 100 g/4 oz French or other green beans, topped and tailed
- 2 skinless chicken breasts (breast halves)
- salt and freshly ground pepper
- 1 tbsp vegetable oil

Dressing
- 1 tbsp finely sliced spring onion (green onion)
- 1 garlic clove, peeled and crushed with a knife or garlic press
- 6 fresh coriander leaves (cilantro), very finely chopped
- 2 tbsp light soy sauce
- 1 tbsp vegetable oil

Beans
Bring a pan of salted water to the boil, add the beans and cook for about 3 minutes or until tender but still crisp. Immediately refresh by plunging into a bowl of iced water, then drain. Keep aside.

Chicken
Cut the chicken breasts crosswise into fine strips and season with salt and pepper. Heat the oil in a non-stick pan and brown the strips of chicken quickly on all sides. Remove and place on paper towels. Keep aside.

Dressing
Combine the garlic, coriander and soy sauce in a small saucepan. Bring to the boil and simmer over low heat for 1 minute, then add the vegetable oil and season to taste. Finally, add the chicken strips and simmer for a further minute.

To Finish
Allow the chicken and dressing to cool slightly, then add the beans and spring onions. Toss gently and serve.

Sweet potato and coriander soup

(Approximately 170 calories per portion)

In this soup the coriander flavour comes mainly from coriander seeds. These are crushed before use so they impart their aromatic oils.

Serves 4

- ½ tsp coriander seeds
- 2 tbsp vegetable oil
- 1 large onion, peeled and coarsely chopped
- 1 garlic clove, peeled and crushed with a knife or garlic press
- 1 tsp curry powder
- 400 g/14 oz (2 cups) peeled sweet potato, diced
- 2 carrots, peeled and diced
- 1 lt/1 ¾ pt (1 qt) chicken stock (see basic recipe, page 190)
- salt and freshly ground pepper
- 2 tbsp plain yoghurt
- 1 tsp finely chopped fresh coriander (cilantro)

Soup
Place the coriander seeds in a fine, clean cloth and crush with a rolling pin or the base of a heavy frying pan. Alternatively, you can grind them in a pepper mill. In a large saucepan, heat the oil, add the onion, garlic, curry powder and crushed coriander seeds and sweat for about 5 minutes or until the onion is translucent, without colouring. Add the sweet potato and carrots and sweat for a further 3 minutes. Add the stock, bring to the boil and simmer for 20-30 minutes.

Allow the mixture to cool slightly, then using a hand blender or food processor, purée until smooth. Pass through a sieve into a clean saucepan.

To Finish
When ready to eat, bring the soup to the boil, season with salt and pepper, and remove from the heat. Add the yoghurt and chopped coriander, and serve.

Mango and Chicken Soup

(Approximately 225 calories per portion)

Chicken and mango harmonize beautifully together, and here they are spiced with the refreshing taste of fresh coriander.

Heat the vegetable oil in a saucepan. Add the shallot and sweat until translucent without colouring. Add the curry powder, white wine and vinegar and bring to the boil. Add the mango, chicken thighs and stock and return to the boil. Simmer over low heat for about 20 minutes. Add the cream and simmer for a further 10 minutes, then remove the chicken thighs from the soup and allow them to cool slightly. Remove the meat from the bone and cut it into fine strips. Keep aside.

Using a hand blender or food processor, purée the soup, then pass through a sieve into a clean saucepan.

To Finish

When ready to eat, bring the soup to the boil and season with salt and freshly ground pepper. Finally, add the chopped coriander and chicken strips, and serve.

Serves 4
2 tbsp vegetable oil
1 shallot, peeled and finely chopped
1 tsp mild curry powder
100 ml/4 fl oz dry white wine vinegar
1 tbsp white wine vinegar
1 small, ripe mango, peeled and coarsely chopped
2 chicken thighs, skin removed
600 ml/1 pt (2 ½ cups) chicken stock (see basic recipe, page 190)
100 ml/4 fl oz single cream (light cream)
salt and freshly ground pepper
1 ½ tsp finely chopped fresh coriander (cilantro)

Shiitake and Smoked Haddock Soup

(Approximately 120 calories per portion)

The distinguished flavour of shiitake mushrooms combine well with the smoky flavour of the fish.

Haddock

Put the haddock in a shallow pan, pour over the milk and water, and cover with a lid. Place over a gentle heat, bring to the boil and simmer for about 8 minutes or until cooked. Remove the haddock from the cooking liquid. Remove the skin and flake the flesh into pieces, making sure all bones are removed. Place the flesh in a bowl and keep to one side.

Soup

Mix the cornflour with 100 ml/4 fl oz of the cold fish stock and keep aside. Heat the oil in a saucepan and sweat the garlic, onion, carrot and leek for about 1 minute over low heat. Add the mushrooms and the white wine and bring to the boil, then simmer to reduce to half. Add the remaining fish stock and return to the boil. Add a little of the boiling liquid to the cornflour mixture, then whisk into the liquid in the pan. Bring to the boil again and skim off any impurities. Add the cream and return to the boil, then add the haddock and season with salt, pepper and cayenne.

To Finish

Sprinkle the spring onion rings and coriander on top and mix in thoroughly. Serve hot.

Serves 4
1 smoked haddock fillet (finnan haddie)
100 ml/4 fl oz milk
100 ml/4 fl oz water
8 tsp cornflour (cornstarch)
1.2 lt/2 pt (5 cups) fish stock (see basic recipe, page 190)
1 tsp vegetable oil
1 garlic clove, peeled and crushed with a knife or garlic press
¼ onion, peeled and finely chopped
10 g/½ oz (1 tbsp) carrot, cut into 2.5 cm/1 inch strips
50 g/2 oz (¼ cup) leek, cut lengthwise into 2.5 cm/1 inch strips
100 g/4 oz fresh shiitake mushrooms, cut into 3 mm/1/8 inch slices
100 ml/ 4 fl oz dry white wine
100 ml/4 fl oz single cream (light cream)
salt and freshly ground pepper
cayenne pepper
1 spring onion (green onion), cut into fine rings
2 tsp finely chopped fresh coriander (cilantro)

Serves 6

250 g/9 oz salmon fillet, skinned and cut into thumb-sized cubes
2 egg whites
50 g/2 oz butter, at room temperature
6 medium-sized asparagus spears
2 medium-sized tomatoes
350 ml/12 fl oz double cream (heavy cream), chilled
2 tbsp Noilly Prat Vermouth
salt and freshly ground pepper
fresh dill and chervil, to garnish

Dressing

2 fresh coriander sprigs (cilantro)
1 tbsp white wine vinegar
¼ tsp English mustard powder
6 tbsp sunflower oil
2 tbsp walnut oil

You will need

6 timbale moulds, each 5 cm/2 inches in diameter, or 6 ramekin dishes, each 7.5 cm/3 inches in diameter.

Oven temperature

140°C/275°F/Gas mark 1

Warm Salmon Timbale with Asparagus

(Approximately 360 calories per portion)

A stunning first course for a dinner party. Although you can check the flavour by tasting a little of the raw mousse during preparation, a truer check is made by poaching a little of the raw mousse in simmering water.

Salmon
Put the salmon and egg whites in the bowl of a food processor and blend until very smooth. Cover the bowl and refrigerate for at least 1 hour.

Moulds
Whilst the salmon is chilling, prepare the moulds. Melt the butter and use about half of it to brush the inside of each mould. Chill until the butter has set, then repeat the process so that the moulds are well buttered and there are no bald spots. Return to the refrigerator until required.

Asparagus and Tomatoes
Snap or cut off the woody ends of the asparagus spears and peel the stalks if necessary. Cut each asparagus spear into 3 cm/1 ¼ inch pieces. Bring a pan of salted water to the boil, add the asparagus pieces and boil for about 5 minutes or until cooked but still crisp. Immediately plunge into a bowl of iced water to refresh; when cold, drain and keep aside. Reserve 3 tbsp of the asparagus cooking liquid for the dressing.

Now prepare the tomatoes. Plunge them into a pan of boiling water for 30 seconds, then immediately into a bowl of iced water until cold. Gently slide off the skins. Cut each tomato into quarters, remove the seeds and cut each quarter into 1 cm/½ inch dice.

Dressing
Remove the leaves from the coriander stalks and finely chop enough to give 2 tsp; keep aside. Place the stalks in a small saucepan and add the reserved asparagus cooking liquid. Bring to the boil, then stir in the vinegar and English mustard. Allow to cool, then strain into a bowl. Whisk in the sunflower and walnut oils. Season with salt and freshly ground pepper.

When the mixture is cold, add the chopped coriander leaves and diced tomato.

Timbales
When the salmon is very cold, return the bowl to the food processor. Working quickly to ensure that the mixture stays cold, blend the chilled cream into the salmon a little at a time. To incorporate the cream properly, you will need to add it in perhaps 4 or 5 batches. Finally, add the Noilly Prat and season with salt and pepper.

Scoop the mixture into a piping bag (pastry bag) and divide among the 6 moulds, filling each about three-quarters full. Try not to trap any air bubbles. In case you have, place a tea towel on the work surface and bang each mould firmly on it. Cover each with plastic film. At this stage you can either cook the moulds to eat in about 50 minutes, or keep them in the refrigerator for up to 4 hours before cooking.

When you're ready to cook, place a few sheets of newspaper on the bottom of a roasting pan. Set the moulds on the paper and pour boiling water into the pan to come about halfway up the moulds. Bake in the preheated oven for 30–40 minutes or until the timbales have risen slightly and are a little firm to the touch. Check by inserting a fine skewer into the centre; it should come out clean. Remove from the oven and leave to rest for 5–10 minutes.

Salmon and Pomelo Parcel

(Approximately 285 calories per portion)

This impressive and tasty first course can be prepared beforehand and plated at the last minute. Pomelo is a citrus fruit that was introduced to me by my friend Charlie Amatyakul. A superb Thai chef, he showed me the versatility of this fruit. You can buy pomelo in good supermarkets or in Asian shops between December and April. As a substitute you can always use grapefruit. However, if you do so, I would recommend that you blanch the grapefruit segments before using them, otherwise they will be too pungent for the dish.

Parcel

Line each teacup with plastic film, overlapping the rim by at least 2 cm/¾ inch. Then line each completely with smoked salmon, overlapping the rim of the cup by at least 1 cm/½ inch. Place in the refrigerator.

Bring the fish stock to the boil in a saucepan. Add the fresh salmon, reduce the heat, cover and poach gently for 5 minutes. Remove from the heat and allow the salmon to cool in the cooking liquid.

When the salmon is cold, remove it from the cooking liquid, reserving the liquid for the sauce. Flake the salmon into small fingertip-size pieces and place in a bowl with the salmon. Cook the celeriac strips in boiling salted water for 30 seconds and refresh in iced water; drain and pat dry with paper towel. Add to the salmon and pomelo.

In another small bowl, mix together the oriental dressing, mayonnaise and coriander. Add to the celeriac, pomelo and salmon and mix gently. Finally, season with salt and freshly ground pepper. Divide the filling into 4 equal portions and spoon it into the salmon-lined teacups. Fold the film together over the top and remove the salmon parcel from the cup. Make sure the salmon joins together by twisting the top to form the shape of a money bag. Tie with a chive stalk. Gently place back in the cups and refrigerate until required.

Sauce

Boil the reserved fish stock until two-thirds of the liquid remains. Add the cream and return to the boil. Add the curry powder and simmer for another 3 minutes, then season with salt and pepper. Remove from the heat and strain. Allow to cool completely.

To Finish

Just before serving, arrange the cucumber slices in a ring in the centre of 4 plates. Remove the parcels from the cups and carefully peel off the film. Place a salmon parcel in the centre of each cucumber ring and garnish the top of the parcel with salad leaves. Stick 2 chive stalks into each parcel. Pour the sauce around and serve.

Serves 4

250 g/9 oz smoked salmon, very thinly sliced
200 ml/7 fl oz fish stock (see basic recipe, page 190)
200 g/7 oz fresh salmon fillet
½ pomelo, peeled and segmented
50 g/2 oz peeled celeriac, cut into fine strips (julienne) (½ cup celery root strips)
2 tbsp oriental dressing (see page 193)
1 tbsp mayonnaise
1 ½ tsp finely chopped fresh coriander (cilantro)
salt and freshly ground pepper

Sauce

125 ml/4 fl oz single cream (light cream)
½ tsp curry powder

Garnish

12 long stalks of chive
½ cucumber (English hothouse cucumber), cut into 3 mm/⅛ inch slices
25 g/1 oz mixed salad leaves such as lollo rosso, curly endive (frisée), chicory (Belgian endive)

You will need

4 teacups

To Finish

Turn the timbales out carefully and place on the centre of each plate. Quickly toss the asparagus into the tomato dressing and spoon the salad around each tin. Garnish each plate with a few herbs and serve.

A WORLD OF FLAVOURS

*Salmon and
Pomelo Parcel
(page 145)*

CORIANDER

Sea Bream Served on an Aubergine Purée

Serves 2

Ingredients
2 sea bream fillets (porgy), each about 175 g/6 oz, scales removed
salt and freshly ground pepper
1 tbsp vegetable oil
sprigs of fresh dill and chervil, to garnish

Aubergine Purée

25 g/1 oz (2 tbsp) butter
1 shallot, peeled and finely chopped
1 garlic clove, peeled and crushed with a knife or garlic press
1 pinch of curry powder
¼ tsp coriander seeds, toasted and ground
1 medium-sized aubergine (eggplant), peeled and cut into 3 mm/⅛ inch slices

Sauce

200 ml/7 fl oz fish stock (see basic recipe, page 190)
100 ml/4 fl oz double cream (heavy cream)
½ tsp chopped parsley
½ tsp chopped fresh basil
½ tsp chopped fresh coriander (cilantro)

(Approximately 605 calories per portion)

Aubergine delicately puréed with a little coriander is an ideal complement to simply pan-fried fish. With a creamy basil and coriander sauce, this is delicious!

Aubergine Purée

Heat the butter in a non-stick saucepan. Add the shallot and garlic and sweat until translucent, without colouring. Add the curry powder and ground coriander and sweat for a further minute. Add the aubergine, season with salt and pepper and sweat for a minute more. Cover with a lid and cook over medium/low heat until the aubergine is completely cooked – it will change colour and become dark. Purée in a blender or food processor and adjust the seasoning if necessary. Keep aside.

Sauce

Bring the fish stock to the boil in a small saucepan. Boil to reduce until half the quantity remains. Add the cream, return to the boil and simmer until a creamy consistency is obtained. Season with salt and freshly ground pepper and keep aside.

Fish

Score the skin of the sea bream 2–3 times with a sharp knife to prevent it from curling up when cooked. Season the fillets with salt and freshly ground pepper. Heat the oil in a non-stick pan and fry the fillets, skin side down first, until they are golden brown on both sides and cooked. Remove them from the pan and keep aside.

To Finish

Gently heat the aubergine purée in a small saucepan and divide it equally into the centre of 2 plates. Place the fillets on top and keep warm. Bring the sauce back to the boil, remove from the heat and add the chopped herbs. If necessary, adjust the seasoning. Pour the sauce around the fish, garnish with a few fresh herbs and serve.

Stuffed chicken breast wrapped in Parma ham

(Approximately 420 calories per portion)

To make the Parma ham easier to handle, keep it refrigerated until required. When complete, the breasts are wrapped in foil to capture all the flavour and keep them moist whilst cooking. Serve this with noodles or mashed potatoes and a green salad.

Stuffing
Mix together the soft cheese, pine nuts and chopped coriander. Season with salt and freshly ground pepper. Place in a piping bag (pastry bag) and keep aside.

Chicken breast
Remove the small fillet from each breast and keep aside. Use a knife to make a cut lengthwise down the centre of each breast, about 1 cm/½ inch deep. From this centre cut, slice into the sides of the breast so as to form a pocket. Pipe an equal amount of the filling into the pocket in each breast. Replace the small fillet on top of the stuffing and press the two sides in lightly. Keep aside.

Spread a piece of plastic film in front of you and place a slice of Parma ham on it. Place a second slice of ham so that it slightly overlaps the first slice, then set a chicken breast on the ham. Lift the film to help wrap the breast in the ham. Remove the film, then brush the chicken breast with oil and wrap loosely in foil. Repeat to wrap the other breasts.

Heat a roasting tray in the preheated oven. Arrange the chicken breast parcels on it and roast for 15-20 minutes or until cooked.

Sauce
In the meantime, prepare the sauce. Heat the butter in a saucepan and add the tomato dices and red wine. Bring to the boil and simmer for 1 minute. Add the chicken stock and simmer for a further 3-4 minutes over medium heat. Season with salt and freshly ground pepper. Add the cornflour to thicken the sauce.

To Finish
Remove the foil from the chicken breasts and arrange them on plates or in a serving dish. Pour the sauce over the chicken, garnish with coriander leaves and serve.

Serves 4

- 4 skinless chicken breasts (breast halves)
- 8 slices of Parma ham
- 2 tbsp vegetable oil
- fresh coriander leaves (cilantro), to garnish

Stuffing
- 75 g/3 oz soft creamy cheese
- 2 tbsp toasted and coarsely chopped pine nuts
- 2 tsp finely chopped fresh coriander (cilantro)
- salt and freshly ground pepper

Sauce
- 25 g/1 oz (2 tbsp) butter
- 1 large tomato, peeled, seeded and diced
- 50 ml/2 fl oz red wine
- 200 ml/7 fl oz brown chicken stock (see basic recipe, page 191)
- 1 tsp cornflour (cornstarch), mixed with 2 tsp cold water

Oven temperature
190°C/375°F/Gas mark 5

Stuffed Chicken Breast Wrapped in Parma Ham
(page 149)

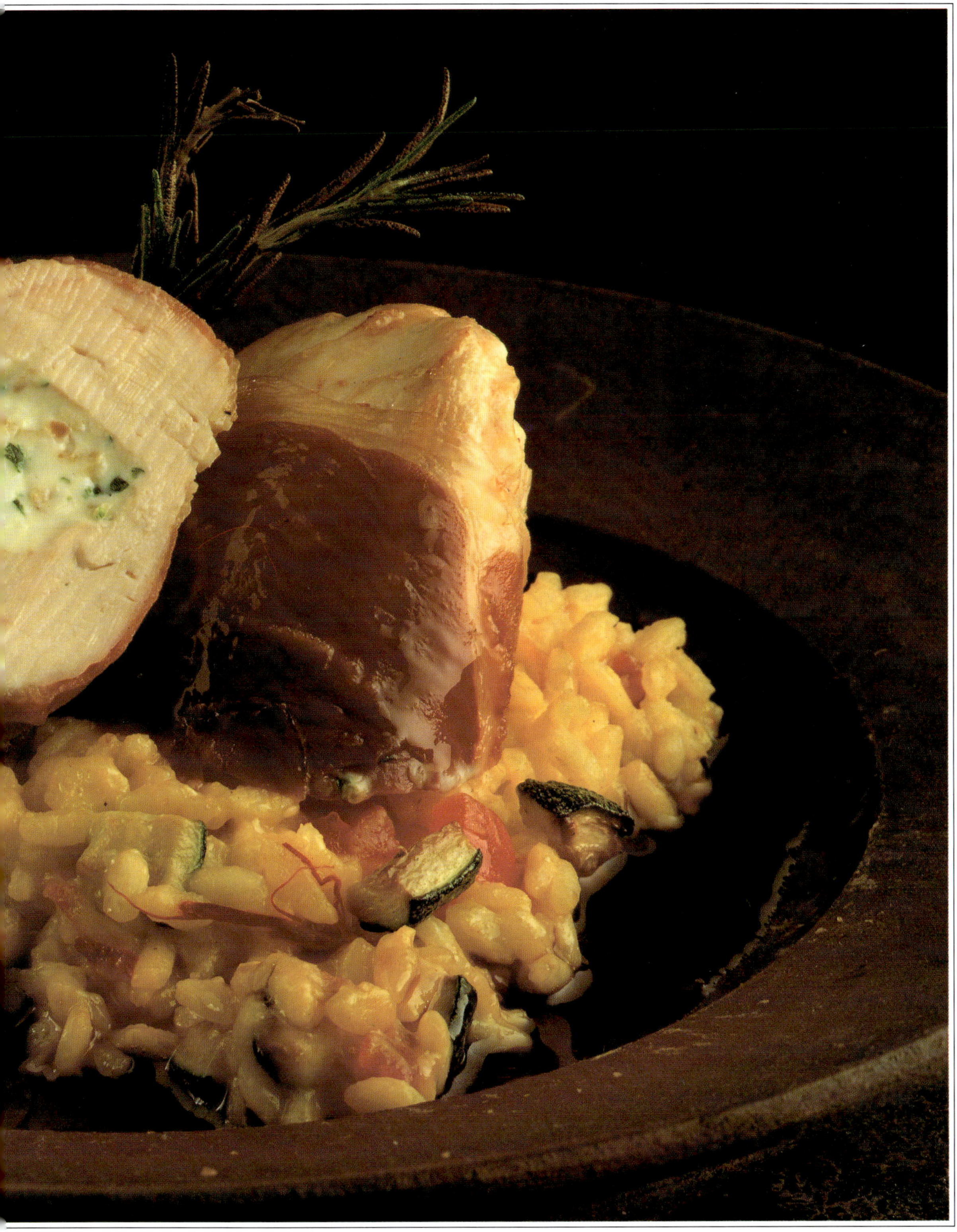

Loin of Lamb Wrapped in a Mousse of Coriander and Bread Croutons

(Approximately 560 calories per portion)

SERVES 4

4 tsp vegetable oil
2 loins of lamb, completely trimmed, about 400 g/14 oz total weight, each cut across in half
salt and freshly ground pepper
100 g/4 oz crepinette (large fresh pieces with no holes), rinsed thoroughly

Mousse

120 g/4 oz boneless lamb (leg or shoulder), fat and sinew removed, chilled
2 egg whites
75 ml/3 fl oz double cream (heavy cream)
3 tbsp vegetable oil
2 slices of white bread, crusts removed, cut into 1 cm/½ inch cubes
25 g/1 oz (2 tbsp) finely chopped shallots
½ tbsp finely chopped parsley
1 tbsp finely chopped fresh coriander (cilantro)

Sauce

1 tbsp vegetable oil
1 shallot, peeled and finely chopped
2 fresh coriander stalks (cilantro)
50 ml/2 fl oz red wine
2 tbsp port wine
300 ml/10 fl oz brown lamb stock (see basic recipe, page 192)
2 tsp cornflour (cornstarch), mixed with 1 tbsp water
15 g/½ oz (1 tbsp) butter
½ tsp finely chopped fresh coriander (cilantro)

Garnish

16 silverskin onions (pearl onions), peeled
8 medium-sized shiitake mushrooms, cut into quarters
16 roast new potatoes (see basic recipe, page 194)
4 sprigs of thyme
4 sprigs of rosemary

Oven temperature

180°C/350°F/Gas mark 4

MEAT
Heat 2 tbsp of the vegetable oil in a non-stick pan. Season the 4 pieces of loin of lamb with salt and pepper and seal in the hot oil to give a little colour on all sides. Remove from the pan and allow to cool. Keep aside.

MOUSSE
Place the chilled lamb in a blender, add the egg whites and blend until smooth. Use a scraper to pass the mixture through a fine sieve into a bowl set in a larger bowl filled with ice. Chill for 3–5 minutes. Fold in the cream a little at a time, then season and refrigerate. Heat 2 tbsp of the vegetable oil in a non-stick pan and fry the bread cubes until golden brown.

Drain on a piece of paper towel and allow to cool. Heat the remaining vegetable oil in a non-stick pan and fry the shallots until translucent, without colouring. Allow to cool. When the croutons and shallots are cool, take the mousse from the refrigerator and gently fold in the parsley, coriander, shallots and croutons, being careful not to break the croutons. Season with salt and pepper.

Place a piece of crepinette measuring about 20x30 cm/8x12 inches in front of you. Spread one-quarter of the mousse on in a 10x12 cm/4x5 inch layer. Place a piece of lamb on the mousse. Wrap the crepinette around the lamb, making sure the lamb is covered by the mousse on all sides and the crepinette is holding the small parcel together. Repeat the process for the other 3 pieces of lamb. Refrigerate for at least 30 minutes.

SILVERSKIN ONIONS
Simmer the silverskin onions in salted water until cooked. Refresh in cold water, drain and keep aside.

SAUCE
Heat the vegetable oil in a saucepan, add the shallot and coriander stalks and sweat for about 30 seconds or until the shallots are translucent, without colouring. Add the red wine and port wine, bring to the boil and reduce the liquid to half the quantity. Add the lamb stock, bring back to the boil and simmer for about 4 minutes. Add the cornflour to thicken, and season with salt and pepper. Pass the sauce through a sieve into a saucepan and keep aside.

LAMB PARCELS
Heat the remaining 2 tbsp of vegetable oil in a non-stick pan over medium heat. Place the parcels in the pan and gently colour on all sides. Remove carefully from the pan to a roasting tray and roast in the preheated oven for 8–10 minutes. Allow to rest for 5 minutes.

TO FINISH

While the lamb parcels are resting, take the same pan you used for browning the lamb, reheat the oil and brown the cooked silverskin onions and mushrooms. Add the roast potatoes and season with salt and freshly ground pepper. When hot, remove the garnish from the pan and place on a paper towel. Keep aside.

Bring the sauce to the boil; remove from the heat and whisk in the butter. Add the coriander. Slice the lamb and arrange on plates, allowing 3 slices per person. Garnish with the potatoes, mushrooms and silverskin onions and pour the sauce around the meat. Finally, arrange the sprigs of herbs around the meat and serve.

Pork steak with glazed goat's cheese

(Approximately 520 calories per portion)

The steaks are marinated to lend a tangy flavour. When cooked, this is complemented by melted cheese and a creamy glaze.

MARINADE

Mix together all the ingredients for the marinade with pepper to taste. Brush the steaks on both sides with the mixture. Leave to marinate for at least 20 minutes.

STEAKS

Heat a roasting tray in the preheated oven. Scrape as much marinade from the steaks as possible, and season with salt. Place on the hot roasting tray and roast in the oven for about 6 minutes on each side or until cooked.

Remove from the oven and arrange 2 slices of goat's cheese on each steak. Then place a slice of tomato on top of the cheese. Season with freshly ground pepper. Mix together the whipped cream, egg yolk and chopped coriander and spoon over the cheese on top of each steak.

TO FINISH

Place the tray under the grill (broiler) for about 30 seconds or until the cream topping has glazed to a golden colour. Then transfer the steaks to plates and serve.

SERVES 4

4 pork steaks (boneless loin chops) each about 175 g/6 oz
salt and freshly ground pepper
8 slices of St. Maurice goat's cheese, or another cylindrical, rindless, firm but not dry goat's cheese, each about 1 cm/$\frac{1}{2}$ inch thick (200 g/7 oz total weight)
1 medium-sized tomato, cut into 4 slices
4 tbsp double cream (heavy cream), whipped
1 egg yolk
1 tsp finely chopped fresh coriander (cilantro)

Marinade

2 tbsp vegetable oil
1 garlic clove, peeled and crushed with a knife or garlic press
$\frac{1}{2}$ tsp English mustard powder
$\frac{1}{2}$ tsp white wine vinegar

Oven temperature

220°C/425°F/Gas mark 7

Grill (broiler)

very hot

A WORLD OF FLAVOURS

Loin of Lamb Wrapped in a Mousse of Coriander and Bread Croutons
(page 152)

CORIANDER

Cod Steak with Tomato Salsa

Serves 4

4 cod steaks, each about 175 g/6 oz
salt and freshly ground pepper
flour to dust
3 tbsp vegetable oil

Tomato salsa

1 tbsp vegetable oil
1 shallot, peeled and finely chopped
1 garlic clove, peeled and crushed with a knife or garlic press
¼ tsp finely chopped fresh hot red chilli pepper (seeded)
¼ tsp tomato purée
100 ml/4 fl oz white wine
4 tomatoes, peeled, seeded and coarsely chopped
1 tsp finely chopped fresh coriander (cilantro)

Oven temperature
180°C/350°F/Gas mark 4

(Approximately 200 calories per portion)

A simple recipe that makes a change from cod and chips! With the tomato salsa and fresh coriander, it is a dish for any occasion.

FISH
Season the cod steaks with salt and freshly ground pepper, then dust with flour. Heat the vegetable oil in a frying pan and fry the steaks on both sides until golden brown. Remove from the pan and arrange in an ovenproof dish. Keep aside.

SALSA
Heat the oil in a saucepan and sweat the shallot and garlic until translucent, without colouring. Add the chilli pepper and tomato purée and cook for a further 2 minutes, stirring constantly. Add the white wine and tomatoes and cook for a further 5 minutes. Season with salt and pepper.

TO FINISH
Pour the tomato salsa over the fish and bake in the preheated oven for 5 minutes. Remove from the oven, sprinkle with the chopped coriander and serve.

Red Mullet and Monkfish Stew

Serves 2

1 tbsp vegetable oil
½ shallot, peeled and finely sliced
¼ garlic clove, peeled and crushed with a knife or garlic press
¼ tsp coriander seeds, freshly ground
100 g/4 oz white of leek, cut into 3 mm/⅛ inch rings
½ celery stalk, 'strings' removed with a peeler, cut into 3 mm/⅛ inch rings
2 tomatoes, peeled, seeded and coarsely chopped
75 ml/3 fl oz white wine
100 ml/4 fl oz fish stock (see basic recipe, page 190)
salt and freshly ground pepper
1 monkfish fillet, about 150 g/5 oz
2 red mullet fillets, each about 100 g/4 oz
6 slices of French baguette, each 1 cm/½ inch thick
1 tsp chopped fresh coriander (cilantro)

Grill (broiler)
on highest setting

(Approximately 520 calories per portion)

In this recipe I use both the seeds and leaves of the coriander plant. The versatility of coriander became apparent to me after working alongside an Indian chef I recall only by his nickname - 'The Medicine Man' - given to him because of his skill with all manner of herbs and spices.

Heat the vegetable oil in a saucepan and sweat the shallot and garlic with the ground coriander, over medium heat until translucent, without colouring. Add the leek and celery and sweat for a further 2 minutes, then add the chopped tomatoes and white wine. Bring to the boil. Add the fish stock, season with salt and freshly ground pepper, and simmer gently for about 5 minutes.

FISH
Meanwhile, skin the monkfish fillet and cut into thumb-sized cubes. Do the same with the red mullet fillets. Add all the fish to the sauce, cover with a lid and simmer very gently over low heat for 3-5 minutes or until the fish is cooked. Adjust the seasoning if necessary.

TO FINISH
Toast the slices of French baguette on each side under the grill (broiler) and keep warm. Sprinkle the chopped coriander over the stew, and serve, with the toasted baguette.

*P*rawns and okra with coriander

(Approximately 170 calories per portion)

Serves 2

2 tbsp vegetable oil
12 raw king prawns (large shrimp), peeled and deveined, heads removed
salt and freshly ground pepper
150 g/5 oz small okra, tops removed
½ onion, peeled and chopped
1 clove garlic, peeled and crushed with a knife or garlic press
1 tsp tomato purée
2 large plum tomatoes, peeled, seeded and diced
100 ml/4 fl oz fish stock (see basic recipe, page 190)
1 tsp chopped fresh coriander (cilantro)

When buying okra (ladies fingers) choose only small ones as larger okra tend to be stringy. Rinse only just before use, then pat dry and pan-fry.

Heat 1 tbsp of the oil in a non-stick pan. Pat the prawns dry with paper towel, season with salt and freshly ground pepper and add to the pan. Reduce the heat and fry on both sides until golden brown. Remove the prawns with a slotted spoon, put on to paper towel and keep aside.

Using the same pan, heat the remaining oil and brown the okra on all sides. Add the onion and garlic and sweat until golden brown. Add the tomato purée and sweat for a further 3 minutes over medium heat. Add the tomatoes and half of the stock, cover with a lid and simmer for about 10 minutes.

To Finish

Add the prawns and remaining stock, season with salt and freshly ground pepper and simmer, covered, for a further 2 minutes. Finally, add the chopped coriander and serve.

*G*ratinated coriander mussels

(Approximately 420 calories per portion)

Serves 4

1 kg/2 ¼ lb fresh mussels
2 tbsp vegetable oil
200 ml/7 fl oz dry white wine
100 g/4 oz (2 cups) breadcrumbs (from 4 slices of white bread)
75 g/3 oz (6 tbsp) unsalted butter, softened
2 garlic cloves, peeled and crushed with a knife or garlic press
2 tsp chopped parsley
2 tsp chopped fresh coriander (cilantro)
freshly ground pepper
25 g/1 oz (¼ cup) Parmesan cheese, freshly grated

Sauce

1 tsp chopped fresh dill
1 tsp chopped fresh coriander (cilantro)
1 medium-sized tomato, peeled, seeded and finely diced
25 g/1 oz (2 tbsp) fresh, cold butter cut into cubes

Grill (broiler)
very hot

These can be served as a main course or first course, or even as a hot snack with drinks.

Mussels

Scrub the mussels individually and remove any 'beard', then rinse twice more in fresh water. Discard any mussels that remain open at this stage. Heat the vegetable oil in a large saucepan, add the cleaned mussels and cook for 1 minute. Add the white wine and bring to the boil. Cover and cook over a high heat for about 5 minutes. Strain the cooking liquid through a sieve lined with muslin or cheesecloth. Divide in half and reserve. Discard any mussels that remain closed, and remove the empty half of each shell from the remaining mussels.

Coriander butter

Combine the breadcrumbs, butter, garlic, parsley and coriander in a food processor and blend together. Season with freshly ground pepper. Spread some of the coriander butter on each mussel in its half shell. Using one portion of the reserved cooking liquid, add ¼ tsp to each mussel and sprinkle with Parmesan cheese.

To Finish

When ready to eat, place the half shells on a baking sheet and grill (broil) for about 3 minutes or until golden brown. Place on a serving dish and keep warm.

Heat the second portion of cooking liquid and add the chopped herbs and diced tomato. Bring to the boil. Remove from the heat and whisk in the cold cubes of butter. Pour this sauce around the mussels and serve.

Serves 4

1 medium-sized duck, about 1.8 kg/4 lb
salt and freshly ground pepper
100 ml/4 fl oz white wine
100 ml/4 fl oz orange juice, strained
50 ml/2 fl oz dry sherry
200 ml/7 fl oz brown chicken stock (see basic recipe, page 191)
3 bananas, peeled and sliced
1 tbsp cornflour (cornstarch)
2 tbsp water
1 tbsp chopped toasted pine nuts
1 tbsp chopped fresh coriander (cilantro)

Oven temperature
200°C/400°F/Gas mark 6

Roast Duck with Banana and Orange Sauce

(Approximately 1080 calories per portion)

Bananas always recall for me a day many years ago when I was temporarily stranded in Arequipa in Peru. Our aeroplane had skidded off the runway on take-off and, whilst waiting for it to be dug out by hand, a local trader did roaring business selling his bananas – the only food available. As I hadn't eaten since the night before, I ate more than I care to remember!

Duck

Place a casserole dish, large enough to hold the duck, in the preheated oven to warm. Season the duck with salt and freshly ground pepper, then place it in the heated casserole. Roast in the oven for about 25 minutes, basting regularly with the duck juices. Then reduce the heat to 180°C/350°F/Gas mark 4 and roast for a further 25 minutes.

Remove the duck from the casserole and drain off the fat. Put the duck back into the casserole and add the white wine and orange juice. Bring to the boil, then add the sherry, chicken stock and banana slices.

Return to the oven and continue roasting for a further 10 minutes, basting frequently, until the duck is golden brown. Remove the duck from the casserole and allow it to rest in a warm place.

Sauce

Mix the cornflour with the cold water. Add a little of the hot sauce to it, then whisk it all into the sauce in the casserole. Bring to the boil and allow to thicken. Cook for 2 minutes. Season with salt and freshly ground pepper, and add the chopped pine nuts and coriander.

To Finish

Remove the wishbone and carve the duck. Serve the sauce separately.

Lemon Grass

I first came across lemon grass in Thailand, and since that first taste of its refreshing, lemony flavour it has become one of my favourite ingredients. The bulbous base and lower stem of this Asian grass is widely used in South-East Asia, especially in curries and stir-fries. The fresh sticks are preferable and are increasingly widely available.

Today the floating market in modern-day Bangkok is a 'must' for tourists. But nearly a quarter of a century ago, when I first visited Bangkok, the floating market seemed caught in time. I'm not sure if the original floating market, just outside the city, still exists, but my memories of it are very clear.

It feels just like yesterday that I was there, on the waterways, or klongs, which are the arteries of life for the people who lived along them. Dozens of fragile boats were loaded with the freshest of produce, all picked in the very early hours and still with dew: papayas or paw paws carefully laid on straw like a regiment of soldiers; countless kinds of vegetables beautifully arranged in wicker baskets. Other boats carried freshly brewed fragrant teas. All was ready for bartering in exchange for a colourful shawl, a plant, or a meal freshly cooked on a floating kitchen that passed by.

My stomach was empty, and I could not resist the aroma of a soup that was simmering in an old dented pot, set over a wood fire in a rudimentary clay oven. The woman tending the soup, her head covered by a traditional straw hat, spooned me a bowl and added some noodles and fresh coriander leaves. What a wonderful flavour it had – quite spicy but so refreshing and slightly lemony. As I was enjoying it, I suddenly bit on a hard stick, which I found looked like a piece of wood. I asked the woman what it was. She turned round in her mobile kitchen, where all her ingredients were carefully laid out in colourful little cups and baskets, and grabbed a bunch of what I now know is lemon grass.

I have come across lemon grass in many parts of Asia since then, and in the ensuing years it has become one of my favourite flavourings. This plant, with its bulbous root end and grass-like leaves, has a delightfully strong lemon fragrance and flavour, a delicious ingredient in soups, curries, meat, fish and many other dishes.

Before using, the outer tougher leaves should be removed. Then you can slice or crush the tender stalk end that remains, or use it whole (in which case, remove it before serving). Very finely chopped lemon grass is delicious in a sauce, as my Malaysian chef, Noreen Scott, showed me.

In some parts of the East, lemon grass is boiled and the liquid drunk as a tea. This gave me the idea of using it to make a flavouring infusion. Simply cut the lemon grass into small pieces, add water and boil for a few minutes. Then strain and add the liquid to any dish of your choice. Start with a little bit first, and add more after tasting.

Lemon grass is now widely available outside Asia, either fresh, bottled, dried in powder form or, as I discovered recently, pickled in jars. I prefer to use only fresh sticks. If I have any left over, I add them to a bottle of sunflower oil and, after a while, I have a lovely lemony flavoured oil to use for salad dressings or to pan-fry fish. Alternatively, any unused fresh lemon grass can be frozen until the next time you need it.

A WORLD OF FLAVOURS

LEMON GRASS

Prawn and Salmon Soup

Serves 4

- 4 raw king prawns (large shrimp)
- 1 tsp vegetable oil
- 100 g/4 oz white of leek, cut into 3 mm/⅛ inch dice
- 2 small new carrots, peeled and cut into 3 mm/⅛ inch dice
- ½ medium-sized fennel bulb, cut into 3 mm/⅛ inch dice
- 300 ml/10 fl oz fish stock (see basic recipe, page 190)
- 200 ml/7 fl oz double cream (heavy cream)
- 1 pinch of ground saffron
- salt and freshly ground pepper
- ½ tsp finely chopped fresh coriander (cilantro)
- ½ tsp finely chopped fresh dill
- 75 g/3 oz salmon fillet, cut into 1 cm/½ inch cubes

Infusion

- 1 tbsp vegetable oil
- 1 lemon grass stick, outer leaves removed, cut into thin slices
- 1 shallot, peeled and sliced
- 200 ml/7 fl oz white wine

(Approximately 310 calories per portion)

To enhance the flavour of this soup I sweat the prawn shells and lemon grass in a little oil. This method can be used in any recipe calling for shellfish – the flavour extracted from sweating the shells will strengthen that of the delicate edible flesh.

Prawns

Peel and devein the prawns; keep the shells but discard the heads. Cut the prawn flesh into 1 cm/½ inch cubes.

Infusion

Heat the vegetable oil in a small saucepan, add the prawn shells and brown them lightly. Reduce the heat, add the pieces of lemon grass and shallot, and sweat for a few seconds. Then add the white wine and simmer until you are left with about half the quantity of liquid. Strain through a fine sieve into a bowl and keep aside.

Soup

Heat the vegetable oil in a large saucepan. Add the leek, carrot and fennel cubes and sweat over medium heat for about 1 minute, without colouring. Add the infusion followed by the fish stock and bring to the boil. Then add the cream, bring back to the boil and simmer for about 5 minutes. Finally, add the saffron and season with salt and freshly ground pepper.

To Finish

Add the cubes of prawn and salmon to the soup. Bring to the boil and remove immediately from the heat. Cover with a lid and leave for 3 minutes. Remove the lid, add the coriander and dill, and serve immediately.

Ham and Papaya Salad

(Approximately 460 calories per portion)

Like all fruit, papayas, or paw paws, need to be well ripened before eating, otherwise the flesh is hard, glassy and lacking in taste. Papayas are normally cut in half, seeds scooped out and eaten in the same way as melon. But the sweet delectable flesh will also complement meat or chicken extremely well, especially dried, salted or cured meats such as the ham in this salad.

Dressing

Combine the white wine, lemon grass stick and vegetable stock in a small saucepan and quickly bring to the boil. Remove from the heat and allow the mixture to cool, then strain through a fine sieve into a medium-sized bowl. Add the mustard and wait until it has dissolved, then add the sunflower oil. Season with salt and freshly ground pepper.

To Finish

Add all the prepared ingredients to the dressing, toss gently and arrange on plates. Sprinkle with the chives and serve.

Serves 4

2 thick slices of lean cooked ham, each about 175 g/6 oz, cut into small finger-sized pieces
½ papaya, peeled, seeded and cut across into 3 mm/⅛ inch slices
50 g/2 oz (⅔ cup) button mushroom, cut into 3 mm/⅛ inch slices
1 small, ripe avocado, peeled and stone removed, cut into quarters and then across into 3 mm/⅛ inch slices
1 tbsp chopped fresh chives, to garnish
Dressing
2 tbsp white wine
½ lemon grass stick, outer leaves removed, thinly sliced
3 tbsp vegetable stock (see basic recipe, page 193)
1 tsp English mustard powder
6 tbsp sunflower oil
salt and freshly ground pepper

Smoked Halibut Salad

(Approximately 215 calories per portion)

Smoked halibut is now easily obtainable in large supermarkets. It can be substituted for smoked salmon and served in the same way, although I prefer it with a salad and sharp dressing.

Wash the salad leaves, tearing the larger leaves in half. Dry the leaves and keep aside.

Cook the sliced carrot in boiling salted water until tender but still crisp. Drain and immediately refresh in iced water. Drain when cold and keep aside.

Dressing

Mix all the ingredients in a small saucepan and bring to the boil. Remove the saucepan from the heat and allow the dressing to cool. Strain into a medium-sized bowl. Adjust the seasoning as required.

To Finish

Add the salad leaves, carrot slices and soya beansprouts to the dressing. Toss together gently, then arrange on plates with the sliced halibut on top of the salad. Garnish with herbs, and serve.

Serves 4

75 g/3 oz mixed salad leaves such as mâche, chicory (Belgian endive), curly endive (frisée)
1 small carrot, peeled and cut into 3 mm/⅛ inch slices
100 g/4 oz (1 cup) soya beansprouts, topped and tailed
250 g/9 oz smoked halibut fillet, finely sliced
fresh dill and chervil, to garnish
Dressing
¼ lemon grass stick, outer leaves removed, cut into fine slices
2 tbsp white wine vinegar
3 tbsp fish stock (see basic recipe, page 190)
4 tbsp sunflower oil
½ tbsp soy sauce
¼ tsp English mustard powder
salt and freshly ground pepper

Smoked Halibut Salad (page 165)

LEMON GRASS

Scallops and Prawns with a Glazed Potato Crown

(Approximately 580 calories per portion)

In 1994, I was challenged by Matthew Kelly on 'YOU BET' to cook within 3 minutes, without any prior preparation, one of seven dishes off The Terrace Restaurant menu. Together with three of my chefs, we completed the challenge with a split second to spare. One of the possible dishes was not dissimilar to this and involved opening scallops and peeling prawns! You won't need to do this, although the recipe will certainly take more than 3 minutes to prepare, but it is worth the effort!

Serves 4

1 tbsp vegetable oil
12 fresh scallops (sea scallops)
12 raw king or tiger prawns (large shrimp), peeled and deveined
finely chopped fresh dill and chervil, to garnish

Sauce

1 tbsp vegetable oil
1 tsp finely chopped lemon grass
½ garlic clove, peeled and finely chopped
100 ml/4 fl oz white wine
200 ml/7 fl oz double cream (heavy cream)
salt and freshly ground pepper
1 egg yolk
2 tbsp double cream (heavy cream), whipped
1 tsp chopped fresh chives

Mashed potatoes

4 medium-large Desiree potatoes or another variety suitable for mashing
50 g/2 oz (4 tbsp) butter at room temperature, cut into cubes
50 ml/2 fl oz single cream (light cream)
grated nutmeg

Grill (broiler)

very hot

SAUCE
Heat the vegetable oil in a saucepan, add the finely chopped lemon grass and garlic, and sweat for 1 minute, without colouring. Add the white wine and boil to reduce the liquid to half the original quantity. Add the cream, bring back to the boil and simmer over low heat for a further minute. Season with salt and pepper. Pass through a sieve into a clean saucepan and keep aside.

MASHED POTATOES
Peel the potatoes, cut into chunks and place in a cooking pot. Cover with cold salted water and bring to the boil. Simmer, covered, until cooked, but slightly under-done, then drain in a colander. Leave for 2–3 minutes to allow the water to evaporate, then press through a potato ricer into a large saucepan. Place over low heat and, using a wooden spoon, mix in the butter cubes one by one. Heat the cream separately and add to the potato mixture. Finally, season with salt and freshly ground pepper and a touch of nutmeg.

Put the potato into a piping bag (pastry bag) and pipe it in a ring on a serving dish. Place under the grill (broiler) until golden brown, then remove and keep warm.

SCALLOPS AND PRAWNS
Heat the vegetable oil in a non-stick pan. Season the scallops and prawns and pan-fry until golden brown on both sides. They should be just cooked. Remove from the pan and place in the centre of the potato crown, arranging them alternately. Keep aside.

TO FINISH
Reheat the sauce gently without simmering and remove from the heat. Whisk in the egg yolk and whipped cream and add the chives. Pour the sauce carefully over the scallops and prawns but not over the potato. Place under the grill and glaze quickly. Finally, garnish with fresh dill and chervil and serve immediately.

Tangy guinea fowl with sweetcorn chutney

(Approximately 290 calories per portion)

Whilst travelling in South America I often came across corn on the cob – most often simply boiled or barbecued. For this recipe, however, I use only the kernels to make a chutney. To remove them easily from the cob use a really sharp knife; stand the cob on its end and slice downwards, keeping as close to the cob as possible. Turn and repeat until all the kernels have been removed.

Chutney

Start by making the chutney, which can in fact be prepared well in advance. Heat the vegetable oil in a large saucepan, add the lemon grass stick, shallots, sweetcorn kernels, red pepper and garlic and sweat for 3 minutes without colouring. Add all the remaining chutney ingredients except for the cornflour and water. Cover and simmer for 30-40 minutes or until the vegetables are tender. Keep aside.

Guinea fowl

About 20 minutes before eating, cook the guinea fowl breasts. Heat the oil in a roasting tray in the preheated oven and add the lemon grass sticks. Season the breasts with salt and pepper and place them on the hot tray. Return to the oven and roast, basting regularly, for 12-15 minutes or until cooked.

To Finish

Reheat the chutney. Dissolve the cornflour in the cold water, then add a little of the hot chutney to it. Stirring briskly, add the cornflour mixture to the chutney and simmer until thickened. Season with salt and pepper. Remove the lemon grass stick.

When the guinea fowl breasts are cooked, remove them from the oven and discard the lemon grass sticks. Pour the hot chutney into a serving dish and place the guinea fowl breasts on top. Sprinkle with the finely sliced spring onion and serve.

Serves 4

1 tbsp vegetable oil
2 lemon grass sticks, outer leaves removed
4 guinea fowl breasts (breast halves)
salt and freshly ground pepper
1 tbsp finely sliced spring onion (green onion) to garnish

Chutney

1 tbsp vegetable oil
1 lemon grass stick, outer leaves removed
3 shallots, peeled and coarsely chopped
1 ear of sweetcorn, kernels removed from cob
1 red sweet pepper, seeds removed, diced
1 garlic clove, peeled and crushed with a knife or garlic press
50 ml/2 fl oz dry white wine
50 ml/2 fl oz white vinegar
200 ml/7 fl oz chicken stock (see basic recipe, page 190)
1 tsp caster sugar (granulated sugar)
½ tbsp mild curry powder
½ tsp English mustard powder
2 cm/¾ inch piece of fresh ginger, peeled and finely grated
½ tbsp cornflower (cornstarch)
1 tbsp cold water

Oven temperature

180°C/350°F/Gas mark 4

A WORLD OF FLAVOURS

Loin of Rabbit and Braised Lentils (page 172)

Loin of Rabbit and Braised Lentils

(Approximately 650 calories per portion)

A hearty and flavourful winter dish. The two loins of the rabbit are tied together, with sticks of lemon grass between them. This imparts a pungent flavour to the sweet flesh.

Serves 2

- 2 saddles of rabbit, each 250 g/9 oz
- salt and freshly ground pepper
- 4 tbsp vegetable oil
- 2 lemon grass sticks, outer leaves removed
- 4 stalks mustard cabbage to garnish (available from oriental shops)

Stock
- 500 ml/16 fl oz water
- 1 lemon grass stick, outer leaves removed

Lentils
- 1 tbsp vegetable oil
- 1 shallot, peeled and finely chopped
- ½ garlic clove, peeled and crushed with a knife or garlic press
- 150 g/5 oz (¾ cup) brown lentils, soaked overnight
- 1 small new carrot, peeled and finely diced
- 6 silverskin onions (pearl onions), peeled

Oven temperature
200°C/400°F/Gas mark 6

Rabbit
Take the loin from each saddle. Reserve the bones for the stock.

Season the loins with salt and freshly ground pepper. Heat half of the vegetable oil in a large saucepan and brown the loins quickly on all sides. Remove from the pan. Use the lemon grass sticks to form a centre 'bone' between the two loins and tie them together with string. Keep aside.

Rabbit stock
Using the pan and oil from browning the loins, add the trimmings and bones from the saddle. Cook until golden brown, then drain off any excess fat. Add the cold water, stock and lemon grass and bring to the boil. Simmer gently over medium heat until reduced to half of the original quantity. Strain and allow to cool.

Lentils
Heat the vegetable oil in a medium-sized saucepan. Add the shallot and garlic and sweat until translucent, without colouring. Add the lentils and the cold rabbit stock and bring to the boil. Cover with a lid, reduce the heat and simmer gently for about 30 minutes or until the lentils are cooked. Add the carrot and silverskin onions. Cover again and simmer until the silverskin onions are cooked. If necessary add more stock or cold water. Season with salt and freshly ground pepper. Remove from the heat and keep aside.

To Finish
Heat a roasting pan or tray in the preheated oven, add the remaining 2 tbsp oil and heat. Add the tied rabbit loin and roast in the oven for 10-12 minutes or until cooked. In the meantime, bring the lentils to the boil, add the mustard cabbage stalks, cover and simmer for 2 minutes or until the stalks are cooked. Remove from the heat. Spoon the lentils on to a serving dish, place the rabbit on top and serve.

Ginger

Ginger is a knobbly root, with a skin that is pale brown in colour and pale yellowish flesh. The flavour is a little hot and slightly woody. The fresh root should be peeled and then finely sliced or grated, or pounded together with other spices. As well as being available fresh, ginger is also sold dried, ground into a powder or, as preferred by the Japanese, sliced thinly and pickled. In addition, you can buy stem ginger preserved in a sweet syrup, which used to be exported from China in decorative jars.

A World of Flavours

GINGER

The very best fish I have ever eaten was a skipjack, caught by line, which was cleaned and then filled with thin slices of fresh root ginger, pale yellowish in colour and not at all fibrous – exactly as ginger should be – before being simply barbecued on an open fire.

This was on Ihuru, one of the Maldive Islands, of which there are more than 1000 (only about 200 of them inhabited). I nearly missed out on that wonderful fish because, having reached Sri Lanka, I was so tired after my voyage from southern India that I wasn't sure I wanted to travel further. My mind felt completely saturated with all the new impressions and the excitement that I had experienced during the previous 2 months of travelling.

Sitting on the verandah of the guesthouse, enjoying the tranquillity and sipping a cup of tea as I watched the sun set, I tried to sort out all the things that had happened and to prepare myself mentally for my trip back home. I pulled out my well-used map, to fix in my mind the names of the villages and places that I had visited. My eyes were drawn to a formation of islands to the west of southern India and Sri Lanka, and I recalled a conversation with a friend some time before. He had raved about the Maldives, calling them an unspoilt paradise! I was so close to them, but wasn't sure that I had the energy left for new places and experiences.

But again, as so many times before, I became restless and something inside me urged me to book a seat on the next flight, of which there was only one a week. What difference would it make? I had travelled so far, I could relax on the beach for a few days and, besides, I did not know when I would be back in this part of the world. So some days later, after about 1 $1/2$ hours of flying through cotton wool clouds, I saw the first of the thousand islands encircled with small coral formations – then another – then one more. What a sight! What excitement! The colour of the sea ranged from a clear light blue to green and finally to a deep blue as the ground dropped away to the ocean floor.

I then had one of the most spectacular landings possible, down on to a small airstrip, built on the islands, that was just long enough for the old propellered plane to land. This was followed by a romantic boat trip on a dohni, gliding over the crystal clear sea to Ihuru, a tiny island so small that I was able to stroll around it in approximately 10 minutes. It was completely unspoilt, with no 'home comforts' at all. Being there made me feel like Robinson Crusoe. Lofty coconut palms fringed the warm lagoon, which was home to spectacular underwater life: rainbow-hued crustaceans, turtles and tropical fish all milling amongst the multi-coloured coral reefs.

After a mind-blowing dive, warmed by the white sand and tropical sun, I felt thirsty and asked the guesthouse owner if I could have something to drink. He pointed to the crown of a coconut tree and before I was able to say anything he had climbed up to collect a coconut. He dropped it to the sand below, came down as quickly as he had gone up, and proceeded to open the coconut very skilfully with a sharp long bush knife. The fresh coconut liquid was delicious and refreshing. What more could I ask for. This was paradise without a doubt.

With three other travellers who were on the island, I enjoyed dinner under a sky packed with glimmering stars, protected by a make-shift roof of coconut leaves. The owner (who was also the chef) offered us the 'chef's speciality' of the day: 'chicken or barbecued skipjack'. Without hesitation I opted for the skipjack and, as I described before, it was sensational. The flavour combination of fish and ginger was enhanced by the smokiness of the open fire. If the fish was this good, I wondered what the chicken would have been like – it was only later that I found out it wasn't available anyway!

A WORLD OF FLAVOURS

GINGER

Red Mullet and
Eel Terrine
(page 180)

Red Mullet and Eel Terrine

(Approximately 310 calories per portion)

This is not a recipe for the novice as it takes some skill and time to prepare. The end result, however, is superb and flavourful.

Serves 10

- 10 medium-sized fresh red mullet fillets, about 800 g/1 ¾ lb total weight, scales removed
- mixed salad leaves
- green asparagus tips, cooked and refreshed
- 8 tbsp oriental dressing (see page 193)
- sprigs of dill and chervil

Filling
- 15 g/½ oz (1 tbsp) butter
- 1 shallot, peeled and sliced
- ¼ tsp finely grated fresh ginger
- 3 tbsp white wine
- 250 g/9 oz red mullet fillet, skinned and cut into cubes (keep refrigerated)
- 1 egg white
- 300 ml/10 fl oz double cream (heavy cream)
- salt and freshly ground pepper
- 1 tsp chopped fresh chervil
- 1 tsp chopped fresh dill
- 300 g/11 oz smoked eel fillet, skin removed, cut into 5 mm/¼ inch cubes

Sauce
- 1 tbsp vegetable oil
- 1 celery stalk, sliced
- 1 shallot, peeled and sliced
- 15 g/½ oz (4 tsp) brown sugar
- 75 ml/3 fl oz white wine
- 2 tbsp brandy
- 150 ml/5 fl oz fish stock (see basic recipe, page 190)
- 175 ml/6 fl oz double cream (heavy cream)
- 3 tbsp bottled creamed horseradish
- 3 tbsp crème fraîche
- 4 tbsp finely chopped fresh chives

You will need
a terrine mould measuring 30x8 cm/ 12x3½ inches, 7 cm/scant 3 inches deep, 1.5 l/2 ½ pt (1 ½ qt) capacity

Oven temperature
110°C/225°F/Gas mark ¼

Filling
Heat the butter in a saucepan and sweat the shallot and fresh ginger over medium heat until translucent. Add the white wine and simmer until all the liquid has evaporated. Allow to cool, and refrigerate to chill.

Terrine
Line the terrine mould with heat-resistant film, or non-stick parchment paper, letting it hang over the edge all around. Line the mould with the red mullet fillets, skin side outwards and slightly overlapping. Let the fillets hang over the edge of the mould. Keep aside.

Place the chilled cubes of red mullet in a food processor with the egg white and the chilled shallot mixture. Blend to a very fine purée. If necessary, pass through a fine sieve. Place in a bowl and chill.

Set the bowl in a larger bowl filled with ice. Stir in the cream slowly until you have a nice smooth mixture. Season with salt and freshly ground pepper. Add the chervil and dill, and gently fold in the smoked eel.

Fill the lined terrine mould with the filling, using a palette knife (metal spatula) dipped in cold water to smooth the top. Fold the ends of the red mullet fillets back over to cover the top. Bang the terrine mould gently on the work surface (covered with a towel) to get rid of any air bubbles. Fold the film over the top, then place the mould in a roasting pan containing hot water. Cook in the preheated oven for 45–50 minutes or until cooked. To test, use an instant-read thermometer: it should register a central temperature of 70°C/158°F. Remove from the oven and allow to cool. Remove from the terrine mould to a tray, still in the wrapping, and chill.

Sauce
Heat the vegetable oil in a saucepan and sweat the celery and shallot until translucent, without colouring. Add the sugar and white wine. Bring to the boil, then add the brandy and fish stock. Return to the boil and simmer to reduce the liquid to half the original quantity. Add the cream and simmer over medium heat for a further 2 minutes. Remove from the heat and pass through a sieve into a bowl. Allow to cool. Add the creamed horseradish, crème fraîche and chives. Season with salt and pepper. Keep aside.

To Finish
Unwrap the terrine and slice carefully into good-size portions. Mix the salad leaves and asparagus with the oriental dressing. Divide the salad equally on to the centre of the plates. Place the slices of terrine on top of the salad and garnish with fresh herbs. Serve the horseradish sauce separately.

Steamed Red Snapper

(Approximately 460 calories per person)

During work experience at The Regent Hotel in Hong Kong, I was able to observe the preparation for a 12-course Chinese banquet for 1000. Knowing from experience how difficult it is to cater for such numbers, I was intrigued to see how they steamed the vast quantity of fish required for one of the courses. With 10 minutes left, bamboo baskets were piled high by a regiment of chefs, then rotated. Finally, the Chinese Master pressed the fish at random to check. Satisfied, he gave the signal to serve.

Mousse
Roughly chop the fish, working quickly to ensure that it remains cold. Put into a food processor with the egg white and blend until a fine purée is obtained. Turn into a bowl and chill.

Set the bowl in a larger bowl of crushed ice. Using a wooden spatula, gradually mix in the cream. Season with salt and freshly ground pepper. Add the ginger and chopped parsley.

Fish
Pierce the skin of the snapper fillets with a very sharp knife. Turn the fillets skin side down on a tray and season them, then use a spatula to spread the mousse gently on top. Put into the refrigerator to chill.

Vegetables
Heat the vegetable oil in a non-stick pan, add the chilli pepper, leek, mushrooms and red pepper and fry for 1 minute. Season with salt and freshly ground pepper, then add the fish stock and bring to the boil. Pour into an ovenproof dish large enough to hold the 4 fillets.

To Finish
Arrange the snapper fillets, skin side up, on top of the leek mixture and next to each other. Cover with a lid and cook in the preheated oven for about 8 minutes, depending on the thickness. Garnish the fish with basil and serve.

Serves 4

4 medium-sized red snapper fillets, scales removed

freshly basil leaves, to garnish

Mousse

100 g/4 oz skinless boneless red snapper, chilled

1 egg white

100 ml/4 fl oz double cream (heavy cream)

salt and freshly ground pepper

¼ tsp finely grated fresh ginger

1 tsp finely chopped parsley

Vegetables

1 tbsp vegetable oil

½ tsp finely chopped fresh hot chilli pepper (seeded)

200 g/7 oz leek, white and pale green, cut into strips

50 g/2 oz oyster mushrooms, cut into strips

1 red sweet pepper, seeds removed, cut into strips

50 ml/2 fl oz fish stock (see basic recipe, page 190)

Oven temperature

200°C/400°F/Gas mark 6

A WORLD OF FLAVOURS

Steamed Red Snapper
(page 181)

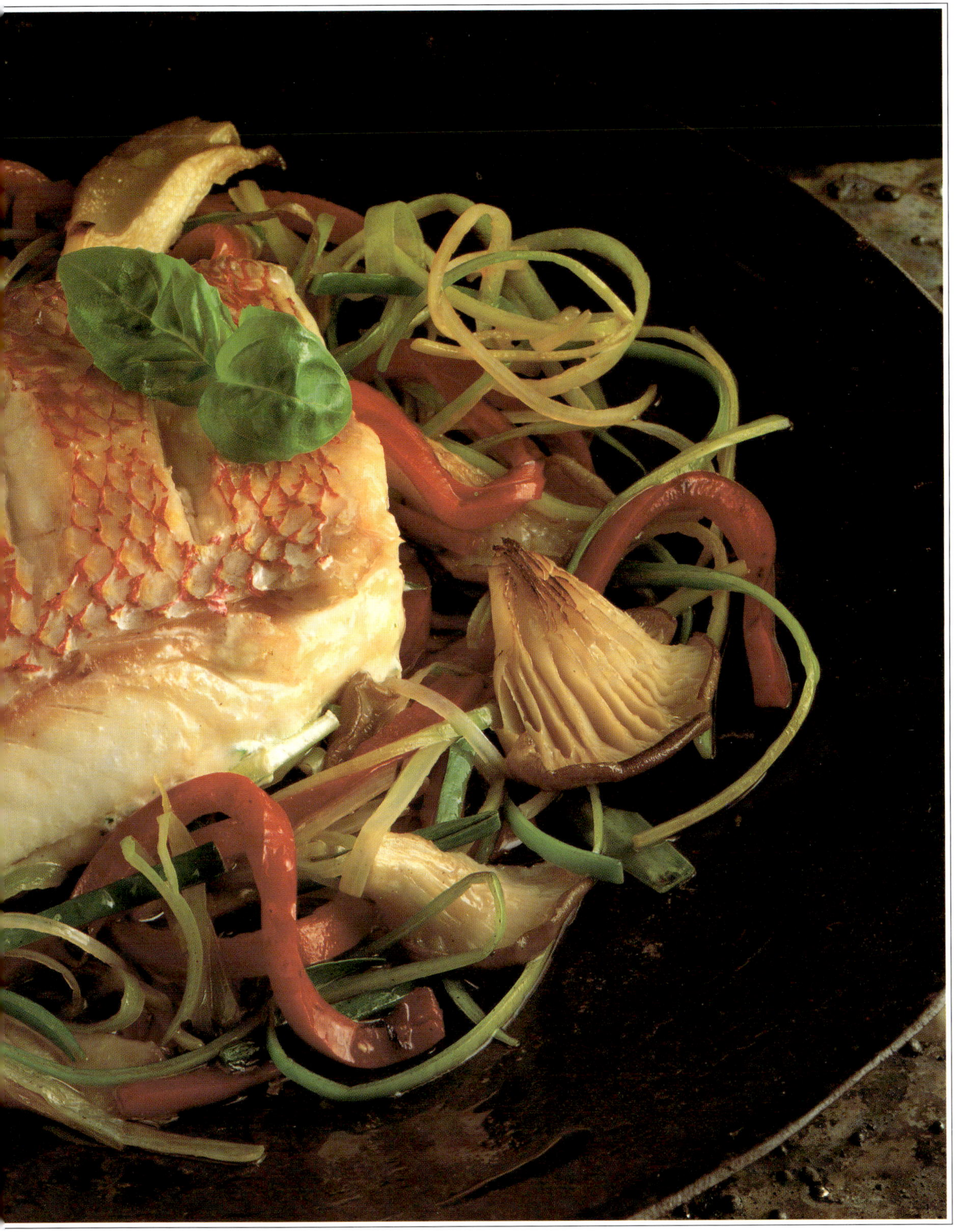

Cold Marinated Breast of Chicken and Vegetables

Serves 4

1 tbsp vegetable oil
2 slices of fresh ginger, cut 3 mm/$\frac{1}{8}$ inch thick, peeled
4 skinless boneless chicken breasts (breast halves)
salt and freshly ground pepper

Dressing

50 ml/2 fl oz sesame oil
$\frac{1}{2}$ garlic clove, peeled and crushed with a knife or garlic press
50 g/2 oz ($\frac{1}{2}$ cup) red sweet pepper, cut into fine strips
50 g/2 oz ($\frac{1}{2}$ cup) yellow sweet pepper, cut into fine strips
25 ml/1 fl oz white wine
75 ml/3 fl oz chicken stock (see basic recipe, page 190)
1 tsp light soy sauce
1 lime, juiced
2 tsp balsamic vinegar
50 ml/2 fl oz sunflower oil

Garnish

50 g/2 oz French or other green beans, topped and tailed
8 spring onions (green onions), cut into 2.5–5cm/1–2 inch strips
$\frac{1}{2}$ tsp finely chopped fresh coriander (cilantro)

Oven temperature

180°C/350°F/Gas mark 4

(Approximately 315 calories per portion)

The ginger in this recipe is used to flavour the oil in which the chicken is cooked. This in turn imparts a delicate hint of ginger to the chicken.

Chicken
Heat the vegetable oil in a non-stick pan and add the slices of ginger. Season the chicken breasts, then add them to the pan and brown on both sides. Transfer them to a baking tray and roast in the preheated oven for about 10 minutes or until cooked.

Dressing
Meanwhile, heat 2 tbsp of the sesame oil in a saucepan, add the crushed garlic and pepper strips and sweat for 1 minute without colouring. Add the white wine and chicken stock, bring to the boil and simmer for 2–3 minutes. Remove from the heat and add the soy sauce, lime juice, balsamic vinegar, sunflower oil and the remaining sesame oil. Season with salt and pepper.

Remove the breasts from the oven and place in a dish that is big enough to hold both the chicken and the dressing. Pour the hot dressing and peppers over the breasts and allow to cool completely. Then refrigerate until required (no longer than overnight). Cook the French beans in boiling salted water. Refresh in a bowl of iced water and drain. Keep aside until required.

To Finish
When ready to eat, remove the breasts from the dressing and cut each one into 5 equal slices. Remove the peppers from the dressing and toss with the beans, spring onions and chopped coriander. Pour the dressing into a serving jug.

Arrange the vegetables on the plates and place the chicken slices on top. If you have a couple of leaves of coriander left, use these to garnish the dish. Serve, handing the dressing separately.

Gingered Prawn and Melon Salad

Serves 4

120 g/4 oz mixed salad leaves such as curly endive (frisée), oakleaf lettuce, mâche, radicchio, lollo rosso
$\frac{1}{2}$ small ripe ogen melon
75 g/3 oz small peeled cooked prawns (small shrimp)

Sauce

$\frac{1}{2}$ lime, juiced
100 ml/4 fl oz mayonnaise
1 tsp white wine vinegar
1 tsp grated horseradish (fresh or bottled)
$\frac{1}{4}$ tsp finely grated fresh ginger
salt and freshly ground pepper

Garnish

finely sliced spring onion (green onion)
radish, cut into fine strips

(Approximately 250 calories per portion)

Salad
Wash and dry the salad leaves, and divide among 4 serving plates or bowls. Cut the melon into 4 wedges, remove the seeds and skin, and dice the flesh into 1 cm/$\frac{1}{2}$ inch cubes. Place in a bowl. Add the prawns and toss together.

Sauce
Whisk together the lime juice and mayonnaise. Add the vinegar, horseradish and ginger, then season with salt and pepper.

To Finish
When ready to eat, gently mix the sauce with the prawns and melon. Divide among the bowls of salad leaves, and garnish with spring onion and radish.

Salmon Roulade served with Soya Beansprouts

(Approximately 625 calories per portion)

During my study period in Thailand I was intrigued by the number of fish used and the treatment they were given. This recipe, using our traditional Scottish salmon, is a result of experimenting and adapting some of what I learnt.

Salmon
Place the piece of salmon fillet between 2 plastic bags. Pound gently to flatten to about 1 cm/½ inch thick, keeping a rectangular shape. Refrigerate.

Filling
Place the chilled salmon cubes and egg white in a food processor and blend until a fine purée is obtained. Remove to a bowl and chill.

Whilst the salmon mixture is chilling, cook the vegetables. Heat the vegetable oil in a pan over low heat. Add the shallot, shiitake mushrooms and ginger and season with salt and freshly ground pepper. Sweat for about 2 minutes without colouring. Remove from the pan and allow to cool. Set the bowl containing the salmon purée in a large bowl of crushed ice. Using a wooden spoon, add the chilled cream gradually until you have a smooth purée. Then add the parsley and cold vegetable mixture. Mix thoroughly and season with salt and freshly ground pepper. Keep in the refrigerator.

Roulade
Remove the flattened salmon fillet from the refrigerator. Spread a piece of heat-resistant film in front of you and place the salmon fillet on top. Season with salt and freshly ground pepper. Remove the filling from the refrigerator and spoon into a piping bag (pastry bag). Pipe the filling lengthwise down the centre of the fillet in the shape of a sausage. Fold the sides of the salmon fillet over the filling and roll into a large roll shape, rolling inside the film. Tie a piece of string around the roll every 4 cm/1 ½ inches. Chill well.

Sauce
Heat the butter in a saucepan and sweat the shallot and ginger for about half a minute without colouring. Add the white wine and fish stock and bring to the boil. Simmer until half of the liquid has evaporated. Add the cream and bring back to the boil. Season with salt and freshly ground pepper. Pass through a sieve into a clean saucepan and keep aside.

To Finish
Cut the film-wrapped salmon roll across into 5 cm/2 inch pieces (2 pieces per person). Heat the oil in a non-stick pan and fry the pieces of salmon roll on both cut sides until golden brown. Remove from the pan to a baking tray. Cook in the preheated oven for about 12–15 minutes or until cooked.

In the meantime, rinse out the non-stick pan and heat the vegetable oil for the garnish in it. Add the cooked asparagus, shiitake mushrooms and beansprouts and heat through. Season with salt and freshly ground pepper. Keep aside. Remove the salmon roulade from the oven and allow to rest for 2–3 minutes before removing the film and string. Arrange the vegetables in the centre of each plate and place 2 pieces of roulade on each. Reheat the sauce and pour around the fish. Garnish with the herbs and sauce.

Serves 4

1 salmon fillet, skin removed, about 350 g/12 oz
2 tbsp vegetable oil

Filling

150 g/5 oz skinless salmon fillet, cut into small cubes and chilled
1 egg white
1 tbsp vegetable oil
¼ shallot, peeled and finely chopped
3 fresh shiitake mushrooms, coarsely chopped
¼ tsp finely grated fresh ginger
salt and freshly ground pepper
100 ml/4 fl oz double cream (heavy cream), well chilled
1 tbsp chopped parsley

Sauce

25 g/1 oz (2 tbsp) butter
½ shallot, peeled and sliced
2 slices of fresh ginger, cut 3 mm/⅛ inch thick, peeled
100 ml/4 fl oz dry white wine
200 ml/7 fl oz fish stock (see basic recipe, page 190)
100 ml/4 fl oz double cream (heavy cream)

Garnish

1 tbsp vegetable oil
4 small asparagus spears, peeled if necessary, cut in half crosswise, cooked and refreshed
8 fresh shiitake mushrooms, cut in half
100 g/4 oz (1 cup) soya beansprouts, tailed
fresh dill and chervil

Oven temperature

190°C/375°F/Gas mark 5

Lamb Casserole with Stem Ginger and Cashew Nuts

Serves 4

- 800 g/1 ¾ lb boneless shoulder of lamb, cut into thumb-size pieces
- 1 tbsp light soy sauce
- ¼ tsp grated fresh ginger
- salt and freshly ground pepper
- 1 tbsp flour
- 3 tbsp vegetable oil
- 2 onions, peeled and finely chopped
- 1 garlic clove, peeled and crushed with a knife or garlic press
- 2 oranges, juiced
- 100 ml/4 fl oz white wine
- 500 ml/16 fl oz lamb stock (see basic recipe, page 192)
- 1 tbsp chopped stem ginger
- 2 tbsp sour cream (optional)
- 2 tbsp chopped fresh coriander (cilantro) (optional)
- 2 tbsp coarsely chopped cashew nuts, toasted in the oven

Oven temperature
180°C/350°F/Gas mark 4

(Approximately 400 calories per portion)

Here I combine both fresh and stem ginger to give quite a unique flavour.

Put the lamb in a bowl. Add the soy sauce and fresh ginger and mix well together. Marinate in a cool place for 30 minutes. Drain the meat in a colander, then pat dry with a paper towel. Season with salt and freshly ground pepper and dust with the flour. (I find the easiest way to do this is to put the flour and seasoning into a plastic bag, then to add the meat and give it a good shake.)

Heat the oil in a non-stick pan and brown the pieces of lamb on all sides. Don't crowd the pan – brown about 6 pieces at a time. Remove the browned pieces with a slotted spoon and put into an ovenproof dish.

Using the same pan and oil remaining in it, sweat the onions and garlic over medium heat until translucent, without colouring. Add the orange juice, white wine and lamb stock. Bring to the boil and pour over the meat. Cover and cook in the preheated oven for about 1 ½ hours or until the meat is cooked.

To Finish

Remove from the oven and add the stem ginger and optional sour cream and coriander. Finally, season with salt and pepper, sprinkle with cashew nuts and serve.

Sticky Banana Pudding

Serves 6

- 50 g/2 oz (4 tbsp) butter or margarine
- 150 g/5 oz caster sugar (¾ cup granulated sugar)
- 1 egg, beaten
- 200 g/7 oz plain flour (1 ⅓ cups all-purpose flour)
- 1 tsp baking powder
- 150 g/5 oz (1 cup) peeled bananas, cut into 1 cm/½ inch slices
- 1 tsp bicarbonate of soda (baking soda)
- 1 tsp pure vanilla essence (vanilla extract)
- 1 tsp finely chopped stem ginger
- 300 ml/10 fl oz boiling water

Sauce

- 225 g/8 oz (1 ¼ cups packed) brown sugar
- 125 g/4 oz (½ cup) butter or margarine
- 100 ml/4 fl oz double cream (heavy cream)

You will need

a round ovenproof dish, 20 cm/8 inches in diameter or 6 ramekins

Oven temperature
180°C/350°F/Gas mark 4

(Approximately 660 calories per portion)

A real old-fashioned winter pudding: stick, rich and in need of great dollops of thick cream.

Cream the butter and sugar together, then add the beaten egg, followed by the sifted flour and baking powder. Mix well together. Combine the sliced bananas, bicarbonate of soda, vanilla and chopped stem ginger with the boiling water. Add to the egg mixture. Turn into the buttered ovenproof dish. Bake in the preheated oven for about 1 hour. For individual puddings divide the mixture into 6 ramekins and place them on a baking tray. Bake for approximately 25 minutes.

Sauce

Combine all the ingredients in a saucepan and bring to the boil, stirring to dissolve the sugar.

To Finish

Remove the pudding from the. Allow it to rest for 5 minutes, then if it has risen slice a thin piece off the top to give a flat base, before turning out on to a serving dish. Immediately pour the hot sauce over. Place under the preheated grill (broiler) until white bubbles form. Serve with thick cream.

Baked Gingered Apples

(Approximately 210 calories per apple)

A very simple yet tasty dessert: the apples are filled with a spicy mixture.

Apples
Rinse the apples and cut out the core using an apple corer. Then use a sharp knife to make a small cut, through the skin only, around the middle of each apple.

Filling
Soak the sultanas in the Calvados for about 10 minutes. Mix the almond paste with the ginger, cinnamon and soaked sultanas. Use this to fill the cavities of the apples. Arrange the apples in a baking tray and seal the top of each cavity with ½ tsp of butter. Finally, sprinkle the sugar over the top. Bake in the preheated oven for 30–40 minutes or until cooked.

To Finish
Make the sauce anglaise according to the basic recipe, adding Calvados or brandy to taste. Remove the apples from the oven and serve warm with the sauce anglaise or vanilla ice-cream handed separately.

Serves 4

4 apples (Golden Delicious)
2 tsp butter, at room temperature
1 tbsp caster sugar (granulated sugar)
vanilla ice-cream (optional)
Filling
50 g/2 oz sultanas (⅓ cup golden raisins)
1 tbsp Calvados
50 g/2 oz almond paste
1 tsp finely chopped stem ginger
¼ tsp ground cinnamon
Sauce
500 ml/16 fl oz sauce anglaise (see basic recipe, page 195)
Calvados or brandy to taste
Oven temperature
200°C/400°F/Gas mark 6

Ginger and Coconut Tart

(Approximately 320 calories per portion)

My friend Sue Bowles once cooked for me a delicious Melk Tert. Since then I've often 'experimented' with her recipe for my own pleasure. This for me is one of my most winning combinations.

Pastry case
Sift the flour into a bowl and rub in the butter. Add the sugar, half of the beaten egg (keep the rest for the filling), the baking powder and salt. Form into a dough, then leave to rest for at least 30 minutes.

Lightly grease the pie plate. Roll out the dough and line the plate. Line with greaseproof paper (wax paper), then place some dried beans into this. Bake blind in the preheated oven for approximately 15 minutes. Remove the paper and beans.

Filling
Combine the milk and chopped ginger in a saucepan and bring to the boil. Add the butter and melt. Mix the cornflour, flour, sugar, salt and desiccated coconut in a bowl and make a well in the centre. Add the eggs (plus the egg remaining from the pastry) and mix thoroughly. Add the coconut mixture to the milk mixture and stir over low heat until thick and creamy.

To Finish
Pour the filling into the pastry case and sprinkle with coconut. Allow to cool before serving.

Makes 1 tart

Pastry case 100 g/4 oz plain flour (⅔ cup all-purpose flour)
50 g/2 oz (4 tbsp) butter
25 g/1 oz caster sugar (2 tbsp granulated sugar)
1 egg, lightly eaten
½ tsp baking powder
1 pinch of salt
Filling
500 ml/16 fl oz milk
¼ tsp finely chopped fresh ginger, or 2 tsp finely chopped stem ginger
15 g/½ oz (1 tbsp) butter
½ tbsp cornflour (cornstarch)
1 tbsp flour
75 g/3 oz caster sugar (6 tbsp granulated sugar)
1 pinch of salt
2 tbsp desiccated coconut (unsweetened dried shredded coconut)
2 eggs, lightly beaten
toasted coconut, to finish
You will need
a pie plate, 18 cm/7 inches in diameter, 4 cm/1 ½ inches deep
Oven temperature
200°C/400°F/Gas mark 6

Stem Ginger and Pear Cake

Makes 1 cake/12 slices

butter to grease pan
flour to dust pan
100 g/4 oz (2/3 cup) currants
2 tbsp Poire Willaim's liqueur
250 g/9 oz self-raising flour (1 2/3 cups self-rising flour)
1 tsp salt
1/2 tsp ground cinnamon
120 g/4 1/2 oz (1/2 cup) butter
150 g/5 oz caster sugar (3/4 cup granulated sugar)
2 eggs
550 g/1 1/4 lb pears
50 g/2 oz (1/3 cup) stem ginger, finely chopped
icing sugar (confectioners' sugar), to garnish

You will need

a round loose-bottomed cake pan, 20 cm/8 inches in diameter

Oven temperature

200°C/400°F/Gas mark 6

(Approximately 270 calories per portion)

After an early start and a couple of hours drive on the way to the Rock of Sigiriya, the local driver stopped and from a road-side stall bought for a few rupees two pieces of cake. The cake contained pieces of crystallized ginger and was strongly flavoured – quite sensational. The combination here with pears is equally memorable.

Line the bottom of the cake pan with greaseproof paper (wax paper). Grease the paper and the sides of the pan with butter and dust with flour. Shake the pan upside down to remove any excess flour.

Mix the currants with the liqueur and leave to soak. Sift the self-raising flour, salt and cinnamon into a bowl. Rub in the butter, then add the sugar and eggs and mix well.

Peel the pears, cut into quarters and remove the core and seeds with a knife. Cut the pear quarters across into 3 mm/1/8 inch slices and add to the cake mixture together with the chopped stem ginger and soaked currants. Fold in to combine well.

Spoon the mixture into the prepared pan and smooth the top. Bake in the preheated oven for 50–60 minutes, then check if the cake is cooked inside. The cake is very moist, so a skewer or knife inserted into the centre will not come out completely clean. Leave the skewer or knife in the cake for 5 seconds, then check to feel if it is hot. Remove from the oven and cool for about 10 minutes before removing the cake from the pan.

To Finish

Place a plate (about 5 cm/2 inches smaller than the cake) upside down on top of the cake. Sift a little icing sugar over the edge to form a border. Carefully remove the plate. Place the cake on a serving plate and serve warm, with cream.

Basic Recipes

Mamdouh's Rice

(Approximately 285 calories per portion)

Firstly, rinse the rice thoroughly, then leave it to soak in fresh water for 15 minutes. Heat the ghee in a medium-sized saucepan. Add the onion, fresh ginger, cardamom pods and cinnamon stick. Cook, stirring, for 3 minutes. Add the turmeric, cumin, coriander, ground cardamom, cinnamon, nutmeg and ground ginger and stir well. (Do not mix the spices together before using.)

Drain the rice and add to the saucepan. Stir for a few minutes to cover each grain with butter and spices, then add 500 ml/16 fl oz of the hot water and the salt. Cover and allow to simmer until about 90% of the water has been absorbed. Stir only once. Then remove from the heat and leave to stand for 15 minutes, still covered.

Add the saffron to the remaining hot water, then add this to the rice. Toss gently with a fork. Cover again and simmer over gentle heat for a further 10 minutes. Remove from the heat and leave, covered, for a further 15 minutes before serving.

Serves 4

250 g/9 oz (1 1/3 cups) basmati rice
25 g/1 oz (2 tbsp) ghee (Indian clarified butter)
1 onion, peeled and finely diced
25 g/1 oz fresh ginger, peeled and cut into large strips
2 whole cardamom pods
1 cinnamon stick
1/4 tsp turmeric
1/4 tsp ground cumin
1/4 tsp ground coriander
1/4 tsp ground cardamom
1/4 tsp ground cinnamon
1/4 tsp grated nutmeg
1/4 tsp ground ginger
600 ml/1 pt (2 1/2 cups) hot water
2 tsp salt
1 sachet saffron (about 12 threads)

Black Bean Sauce

Serves 4

- 1 finger-size strip of dried mandarin peel
- 1 tbsp vegetable oil
- 2 garlic cloves, peeled and finely chopped
- 40 g/1 ½ oz finely chopped Chinese fermented black beans
- ¼ tsp corn oil
- 1 tbsp sugar
- 2 tbsp oyster sauce
- 1 tbsp shaoxing rice wine
- 1 tbsp dark soy sauce
- 1 tbsp sesame oil
- 1 tsp cornflour (cornstarch), mixed with 3 tbsp cold water

Soak the dried mandarin peel in cold water for about 1 hour or until soft, then drain and chop finely. Keep aside.

Heat the vegetable oil in a saucepan, add the garlic and sweat for about 1 minute without colouring. Add the chopped black beans, reduce the heat and sweat for another 2 minutes. Remove from the heat and add all the other ingredients, except the cornflour. Bring to the boil and simmer very gently for 10 minutes.

Stir the cornflour and water mixture, then, whisking vigorously, add to the hot sauce. Simmer gently until thickened. Season with salt.

Allow to cool, then pour the sauce into a sterilized jar. It will keep for up to 1 week in the refrigerator.

Fish Stock

Makes 1 lt/1 ¾ pt (1 qt)

- 1 kg/2 ¼ lb white fish bones (from sole, turbot), broken up
- 2 tbsp vegetable oil
- 50 g/2 oz (⅛ cup) peeled onions, cut into 1 cm/½ inch cubes
- 50 g/2 oz (⅛ cup) white of leek, cut into 1 cm/½ inch cubes
- 25 g/1 oz (2 tbsp) peeled celeriac (celery root), cut into 1 cm/½ inch cubes
- 25 g/1 oz button mushrooms
- 100 ml/4 fl oz dry white wine
- 1 ¼ lt/2 pt (5 cups) water
- 1 sprig of fresh thyme
- ¼ bay leaf
- 1 sprig of fresh dill
- salt and freshly ground white pepper

Thoroughly wash the fish bones, discarding the head and any skin.

Heat the vegetable oil in a large saucepan and sweat the cut vegetables and the mushrooms over gentle heat. Add the fish bones, white wine, cold water and herbs, then bring slowly to the boil. Skim off any impurities with a ladle. Allow to simmer for 20 minutes, skimming occasionally.

Strain through muslin or cheesecloth, or a fine sieve, using a ladle. (It is important not to pour the liquid through the sieve as the stock will then become cloudy.) Season with salt and white pepper and allow to cool.

To store, pour into a sterilized jar, close tightly with a lid and keep in the refrigerator for up to 4 days. When required, pour back into a pot and bring to the boil. Alternatively, if you're not planning on using it immediately or within 4 days, pour into ice cube trays and freeze. Then simply pop cubes out of the trays and store in a plastic bag or container to use as required.

Chicken Stock

Makes 1 lt/1 ¾ pt (1 qt)

- 1 kg/2 ¼ lb poultry bones and wingtips or wings, or 1 boiling fowl
- 2 lt/3 ½ pt (2 qt) cold water
- 50 g/2 oz (⅓ cup) peeled onions, cut into 1 cm/½ inch cubes
- 50 g/2 oz (⅓ cup) white of leek, cut into 1 cm/½ inch pieces
- 25 g/1 oz (2 tbsp) celery or peeled celeriac (celery root), cut into 1 cm/½ inch pieces
- 1 sprig of fresh rosemary
- ¼ bay leaf
- 4 white peppercorns, crushed
- salt

White chicken stock is mainly use for soups and when you wish to keep a sauce white in colour, for example in a fricassée, in vol-au-vent fillings and the traditional way of cooking a blanquette.

Place the bones and wings or boiling fowl in a large saucepan. Add the cold water and bring to the boil slowly. Skim off any impurities.

Add the vegetables, herbs and peppercorns. Simmer gently for 1–1 ½ hours, occasionally removing any impurities and fat with a ladle.

Strain the stock through muslin or cheesecloth, or a fine sieve, using a ladle. (It is important not to pour the liquid through the sieve as the stock will then become cloudy.) Season with salt. Allow to cool.

To store, pour into a sterilized jar, close tightly with a lid and keep in the refrigerator for up to 4 days. When required, pour back into a pot and bring to the boil. Alternatively, if you're not planning on using it immediately or within 4 days, pour into ice cube trays and freeze. Then simply pop cubes out of the trays and store in a plastic bag or container to use as required.

Brown Chicken Stock

Heat the vegetable oil in a roasting pan, add the bones or wingtips and roast in the preheated oven until brown. Add the vegetables and continue to roast for 4-5 minutes. Add the tomato purée and roast for a further 3 minutes. Remove from the oven and drain in a colander to remove any fat.

Transfer to a saucepan and add 200 ml/7 fl oz of the cold water or chicken stock. Bring to the boil and reduce to a consistency that will coat the back of a spoon, stirring constantly. Add the tomato, herbs, peppercorns and remaining water or chicken stock and return to the boil. Simmer gently for 1 ½-2 hours. Remove any impurities or fat occasionally with a ladle.

Strain the stock through muslin or cheesecloth, or a fine sieve, using a ladle. (It is important not to pour the liquid through the sieve as the stock will then become cloudy.) Season with salt. Allow to cool.

To store, pour into a sterilized jar, close tightly with a lid and keep in the refrigerator for up to 4 days. When required, pour back into a pot and bring to the boil. Alternatively, if you're not planning on using it immediately or within 4 days, pour into ice cube trays and freeze. Then simply pop cubes out of the trays and store in a plastic bag or container to use as required.

Makes 1 lt/1 ¾ pt (1 qt)

50 ml/2 fl oz vegetable oil
1 kg/2 ¼ lb chicken bones, cut into small pieces, or wingtips or wings
50 g/2 oz (⅓ cup) peeled onion, cut into 1 cm/½ inch cubes
25 g/1 oz (2 tbsp) celery or peeled celeriac (celery root), cut into 1 cm/½ inch cubes
25 g/1 oz (¼ cup) carrot, cut into 1 cm/½ inch cubes
1 tsp tomato purée
2 lt/3 ½ pt (2 qt) cold water or chicken stock (see basic recipe, opposite)
100 g/4 oz (½ cup) tomato, diced
1 sprig of fresh rosemary
¼ bay leaf
4 white peppercorns, crushed
salt

Oven temperature
180°C/350°F/Gas mark 4

Brown Veal Stock

Heat the oil in a roasting pan and add the veal bones and calf's feet pieces. Roast in the preheated oven until brown. Add the vegetables and continue to roast for 4-5 minutes. Add the tomato purée and roast for a further 3 minutes. Remove from the oven and drain in a colander to remove the fat.

Transfer to a saucepan, add 500 ml/16 fl oz of the water and bring to the boil. Reduce to a consistency that will coat the back of a spoon, stirring constantly. Add the tomato, herbs, peppercorns and remaining water. Return to the boil and simmer gently for 1 ½-2 hours, removing any impurities or fat with a ladle occasionally.

Strain the stock through muslin or cheesecloth, or a fine sieve, using a ladle. (It is important not to pour the liquid through the sieve as the stock will then become cloudy.) Season with salt. Allow to cool.

To store, pour into a sterilized jar, close tightly with a lid and keep in the refrigerator for up to 4 days. When required, pour back into a pot and bring to the boil. Alternatively, if you're not planning on using it immediately or within 4 days, pour into ice cube trays and freeze. Then simply pop cubes out of the trays and store in a plastic bag or container to use as required.

Makes 1 lt/1 ¾ pt (1 qt)

50 ml/2 fl oz vegetable oil
800 g/1 ¾ lb veal bones, cut into small pieces, or trimmings
200 g/7 oz calf's feet cut into small pieces
50 g/2 oz (⅓ cup) peeled onions, cut into 1 cm/½ inch pieces
25 g/1 oz (2 tbsp) peeled celeriac (celery root) or celery, cut into 1 cm/½ inch pieces
25 g/1 oz (¼ cup) carrot, cut into 1 cm/½ inch pieces
1 tsp tomato purée
2 lt/3 ½ pt (2 qt) water
100 g/4 oz (½ cup) tomato, diced
¼ bay leaf
1 sprig of fresh thyme
1 sprig of fresh rosemary
4 white peppercorns, crushed
salt

Oven temperature
180°C/350°F/Gas mark 4

Veal Glace

Makes 200 ml/7 fl oz

1 lt/1 ¾ pt (1 qt) brown veal stock (see basic recipe, page 191)
salt

The same recipe can be used for other glaces by substituting the relevant stock such as chicken, fish, lamb or game. If you intend to use your stocks for glaces, remember not to season with salt until after the reduction.

Put the stock in a large saucepan and bring to the boil. Simmer gently until reduced to half the quantity. Remove any impurities with a ladle. Strain through a muslin or cheesecloth into a small saucepan and boil to reduce again to half the quantity. Season with salt, then allow to cool.

To store, pour into a sterilized jar, close tightly with a lid and keep in the refrigerator for up to 4 days. When required, pour back into a pot and bring to the boil. Alternatively, if you're not planning on using it immediately or within 4 days, pour into ice cube trays and freeze. Then simply pop cubes out of the trays and store in a plastic bag or container to use as required.

Lamb Stock

Makes 1 lt/1 ¾ pt (1 qt)

1 kg/2 ¼ lb lamb bones or trimmings
2 lt/3 ½ pt (2 qt) water
50 g/2 oz (⅓ cup) peeled onion, cut into 1 cm/½ inch pieces
50 g/2 oz (⅓ cup) white of leek, cut into 1 cm/⅛ inch pieces
25 g/1 oz (2 tbsp) celery or (celery root) celeriac, cut into 1 cm/½ inch pieces
1 sprig of fresh thyme
¼ bay leaf
4 white peppercorns, crushed
salt

Put the lamb bones in a pan of cold water, bring to the boil and drain. Return the bones to the pot, add the measured water and bring slowly to the boil. Skim as required to remove any impurities.

Add the vegetables, herbs and peppercorns. Simmer gently for about 1 hour, occasionally removing any impurities and fat with a ladle.

Strain the stock through muslin or cheesecloth, or a fine sieve, using a ladle. (It is important not to pour the liquid through the sieve as the stock will then become cloudy.) Season with salt. Allow to cool.

To store, pour into a sterilized jar, close tightly with a lid and keep in the refrigerator for up to 4 days. When required, pour back into a pot and bring to the boil. Alternatively, if you're not planning on using it immediately or within 4 days, pour into ice cube trays and freeze. Then simply pop cubes out of the trays and store in a plastic bag or container to use as required.

Brown Lamb Stock

Makes 1 lt/1 ¾ pt (1 qt)

50 ml/2 fl oz vegetable oil
800 g/1 ¾ lb lamb bones, chopped
200 g/7 oz lamb trimmings
50 g/2 oz (⅓ cup) peeled onion, cut into 1 cm/½ inch cubes
25 g/1 oz (2 tbsp) peeled celeriac (celery root) or celery, cut into 1 cm/½ inch cubes
25 g/1 oz (¼ cup) carrot, cut into 1 cm/½ inch cubes
1 tsp tomato purée
2 lt/3 ½ pt (2 qt) water or lamb stock (see basic recipe, above)
100 g/4 oz (½ cup) tomato, diced
¼ bay leaf
1 sprig of fresh thyme
4 white peppercorns, crushed
salt

Oven temperature
180°C/350°F/Gas mark 4

Heat the vegetable oil in a roasting pan, add the lamb bones and trimmings and roast in the preheated oven until brown. Add the vegetables and continue to roast for 4–5 minutes. Then add the tomato purée and roast for a further 3 minutes. Remove from the oven and drain in a colander to remove the fat.

Transfer to a saucepan. Add 500 ml/16 fl oz of the water or lamb stock and bring to the boil. Reduce to a consistency that will coat the back of a spoon, stirring constantly. Add the tomato, herbs, peppercorns and remaining water or stock. Bring to the boil and simmer gently for 1 ½–2 hours, removing any impurities or fat with a ladle as required.

Strain the stock through muslin or cheesecloth, or a fine sieve, using a ladle. (It is important not to pour the liquid through the sieve as the stock will then become cloudy.) Season with salt. Allow to cool.

To store, pour into a sterilized jar, close tightly with a lid and keep in the refrigerator for up to 4 days. When required, pour back into a pot and bring to the boil. Alternatively, If you're not planning on using it immediately or within 4 days, pour into ice cube trays and freeze. Then simply pop cubes out of the trays and store in a plastic bag or container to use as required.

Vegetable Stock

Heat the vegetable oil in a medium-sized saucepan and sweat the onion, leek, celery, cabbage and garlic for about 2 minutes without colouring. Then add the tomato, bay leaf, peppercorns and cold water and bring to the boil. Allow to simmer for about 1 hour, then season with salt.

Remove from the heat and strain through a fine sieve, pressing on the vegetables to release as much liquid as possible. Allow to cool, and use as required.

To store, pour into a sterilized jar, close tightly with a lid and keep in the refrigerator for up to 4 days. When required, pour back into a pot and bring to the boil. Alternatively, if you're not planning on using it immediately or within 4 days, pour into ice cube trays and freeze. Then simply pop cubes out of the trays and store in a plastic bag or container to use as required.

Makes 1 lt/1 ¾ pt (1 qt)

2 tbsp vegetable oil
1 small onion, peeled and sliced
1 small white of leek, sliced
100 g/4 oz celery, diced
100 g/4 oz cabbage, shredded
1 garlic clove, peeled and sliced
¼ bay leaf 5 white peppercorns, crushed
1.5 lt/2 ¼ pt (1 ½ qt) water
salt

Mashed Potatoes

Peel the potatoes, cut into chunks and place in a cooking pot. Cover with cold water and bring to the boil. Simmer, covered, until cooked but slightly underdone. Drain in a colander and leave for 2–3 minutes, to allow the remaining water to evaporate, then press through a potato ricer into a larger saucepan. Place over low heat and, using a wooden spoon, mix in the butter cubes one by one. Heat the cream separately and add to the potato mixture. Finally, season with salt, freshly ground pepper and a touch of nutmeg.

Serves 4

4 medium-sized red-skinned potatoes, such as Desiree, about 400 g/ 14 oz in total
50 g/2 oz (4 tbsp) butter, cut into small cubes
50 ml/2 fl oz single cream (light cream)
salt and freshly ground white pepper
grated nutmeg

Curry Sauce for Fish

This sauce can just as easily be used for vegetables, veal or chicken. Simply substitute the relevant stock.

Melt the butter in a saucepan, then add the shallots and lemon grass. Sweat until the shallots are translucent, without colouring. Stir in the spices, bay leaf peppercorns and garlic and allow to cool.

Add the white wine and bring to the boil. Simmer gently to reduce to half the quantity. Add the fish stock and oyster sauce. Return to the boil and reduce again to half the quantity. Finally, add the coconut cream and the cream and boil to reduce to a creamy consistency. Season with salt, freshly ground pepper and Tabasco. Pass the sauce through a sieve.

Makes 1 lt/1 ¾ pt (1 qt)

15 g/½ oz (1 tbsp) butter
200 g/7 oz shallots, peeled and finely chopped
15 g/½ oz lemon grass, outer leaves removed, sliced
1 ½ tsp mild curry powder
¼ tsp turmeric
½ tsp coriander seeds
2 cloves
3 whole cardamom pods
¾ tsp grated fresh ginger
½ bay leaf
40 white peppercorns
1 garlic clove, peeled and crushed with a knife or garlic press
100 ml/4 fl oz white wine
300 ml/10 fl oz fish stock (see basic recipe, page 190)
¾ tsp oyster sauce
100 ml/4 fl oz canned unsweetened coconut cream (thick coconut milk)
800 ml/1 ⅓ pt double cream (3 ¼ cups heavy cream)
salt and freshly ground white pepper
Tabasco sauce

Roast Potatoes

Serves 4

24 medium-sized new potatoes, about 500 g/1 lb 2 oz total weight
vegetable oil
1 sprig of fresh rosemary
salt and freshly ground pepper

Oven temperature
200°C/400°F/Gas mark 6

Bring some water to the boil in a saucepan large enough to hold the potatoes comfortably. In the meantime, peel the potatoes. When the water is boiling, drop in the potatoes and boil for 3–4 minutes. Drain in a colander, then spread put on a tray, making sure they do not lie on top of each other. Their own heat will make any excess water evaporate. Allow the potatoes to cool.

Heat a roasting or baking pan that is large enough to hold the potatoes in a single layer, in the preheated oven. Add the vegetable oil and, when hot, add the potatoes and rosemary. Roast in the oven for about 15 minutes, depending on their size, until cooked, crisp and golden brown. Season the potatoes with salt. Use slotted spoon to transfer to a serving dish and serve immediately.

Orange Sauce

Makes 500 ml/16 fl oz

3 tbsp caster sugar (granulated sugar)
50 ml/2 fl oz Grand Marnier
500 ml/16 fl oz orange juice
¼ tsp finely grated fresh ginger
¼ tsp ground cinnamon
3 tbsp orange marmalade
2 tbsp cornflour (cornstarch), mixed with 3 tbsp cold water

Put the sugar in a saucepan and heat over medium heat until melted and golden brown. Do not stir! Also, be sure that the heat source is the same size as the base of the pan, so the sugar will melt evenly. Remove the saucepan from the heat and allow the melted sugar to cool. (It will harden but will liquefy again when the other ingredients are added.) Then add the Grand Marnier, orange juice, ginger, cinnamon powder and marmalade and bring back to the boil. Simmer for about 5 minutes. Add the cornflour mixture and simmer again until the sauce has thickened. Pass the sauce through a sieve and use either hot or cold.

Chocolate Sauce

Serves 6

150 ml/5 fl oz milk
150 g/5 oz best-quality confectioner's bittersweet chocolate

Chop the chocolate coarsely and keep aside.

Heat the milk in a saucepan and bring to the boil. Add the chopped chocolate and mix together with a whisk until the chocolate has melted and the sauce is smooth. Do not boil. Remove from the heat and use as required, hot or cold.

If you feel the sauce is too thick, simply dilute it with a little cold milk.

Raspberry Sauce

Makes approx 500 ml/16 fl oz

250 g/9 oz (2 cup) fresh, ripe raspberries
250 g/9 oz icing sugar (2 cups confectioners' sugar)
125 ml/4 ½ fl oz water

Combine all the ingredients in a saucepan. Bring slowly to the boil, and simmer for 2 minutes. Purée the mixture in a food processor or blender, then pass through a sieve. Serve warm or allow to cool.

The sweetness of raspberries can vary, so if you wish to sweeten the sauce further, shake a little icing sugar into it at the end.

Sauce Anglaise

Put the milk in a heavy-based saucepan, add the vanilla pod and bring to the boil. Beat the egg yolks with the sugar until slightly foamy, then gradually add the hot milk, whisking constantly. Pour back into the pan and heat slowly, stirring with a wooden spoon. Do not allow to boil or the mixture will separate. Continue to heat slowly, stirring, until the sauce thickens enough to coat the back of the wooden spoon. Immediately remove from the heat and strain through a fine sieve. Finally, add the cream. Serve hot or allow to cool and use as required.

Makes about 750 ml/1 1/4 pt (3 cups)

- 500 ml/16 fl oz milk
- 1 vanilla pod (vanilla bean) split in half lengthwise
- 5 egg yolks
- 100 g/4 oz caster sugar (1/2 cup granulated sugar)
- 150 ml/5 fl oz double cream (heavy cream)

Vanilla Sponge

Put the eggs and sugar in a bowl and set over a bowl of hot water. Whisk to the ribbon stage: to check, lift the mixture with the whisk and draw a figure 8 on the surface. If it holds this shape for a few seconds, it is ready. Remove the bowl from the heat and continue whisking until the mixture is cold. Sift the flour and gently fold into the mixture. Finally, add the melted butter. Pour the mixture into the well-greased and floured pan. Bake in the oven for 30–35 minutes. Remove from the oven and place the pan on a wire rack to cool. Remove from the pan when cold, using a knife to loosen if necessary.

Makes an 18 cm/7 inch round sponge

- butter and flour for the pan
- 4 eggs
- 150 g/5 oz caster sugar (3/4 cup granulated sugar)
- 150 g/5 oz plain flour (1 1/4 cups cake flour)
- 50 g/2 oz (4 tbsp) butter, melted

You will need

a round cake pan, 18 cm/7 inches in diameter

Oven temperature

200°C/400°F/Gas mark 6

Sweet Pastry

Beat the butter with the sugar until pale and creamy. Mix in the egg yolk. Add the flour and mix until a smooth dough is formed. Allow it to rest in the refrigerator for at least 15 minutes before using.

Makes 300 g/11 oz

- 100 g/4 oz (1/2 cup) unsalted butter, at room temperature, cut into cubes
- 50 g/2 oz caster sugar (1/4 cup granulated sugar)
- 1 egg yolk
- 150 g/5 oz plain white flour (1 cup all-purpose flour)

Shortcrust Pastry

I find the easiest way to make this is using a food processor. However, if you don't have one it can also be made quite quickly by hand, as explained here.

Place the flour, baking powder and salt in a bowl. Cut the butter into small pieces and lightly rub it in with your fingertips until the mixture resembles fine breadcrumbs. Using a fork, mix in the lightly beaten egg yolk and enough milk to form a smooth dough. Allow it to rest in the refrigerator for at least 15 minutes before using.

Makes 250 g/9 oz

- 150 g/5 oz plain flour (1 cup all-purpose flour)
- 1/2 tsp baking powder
- salt
- 75 g/3 oz (6 tbsp) unsalted butter
- 1 egg yolk, lightly beaten
- 50 ml/2 fl oz milk

Index

A
Apricot Crumble 50
Aubergine and Smoked Mackerel 42
Aubergine Soup 40
aubergines
  Aubergine Soup 40
  Aubergines and Smoked Mackerel 42
  Monkfish and Prawns with Aubergines and Plum Tomatoes 77
  Sea Bream Served on Aubergine Purée 148

B
Baked Gingered Apples 187
Banana Crumble with Passion Fruit and Coconut 30
bananas
  Banana Crumble with Passion Fruit and Coconut 30
  Roast Duck with Banana and Orange Sauce 158
  Sticky Banana Pudding 186
beans and pulses
  Black Bean Sauce 190
  Chicken and French Bean Salad 142
  Loin of Rabbit and Braised Lentils 172
  Monkfish with Beansprouts and Mangetout 91
  Rabbit and Braised Lentils 172
  Red Lentil and Clam Soup 89
  Red Mullet with Black Beans and Mashed Potatoes 73
beef
  Sirloin Steak with Black Olive Sauce 61
  Sirloin Steak with Horseradish Relish 82
  Steak with Sweet Potato Sauce 45
Black Bean Sauce 190
Broccoli and Cauliflower Timbale 76

C
cakes and gâteaux
  Mango gâteau 29
  Pumpkin and Cashew Nut Cake 49
  Pumpkin and Coconut Cake 100
  Stem Ginger and Pear Cake 188
  Vanilla Sponge 195
Caramelized Onion and Cottage Cheese Tart 18, 20
cardamom 13, 16–17
Cardamom Rice with Chicken and Fish 25, 26
Cardamom-flavoured Peach Gratin 30
Celeriac and Chestnut Soup 88
cheese
  Caramelized Onion and Cottage Cheese Tart 20
  Pork Steak with Glazed Goat's Cheese 152
  Ricotta Cheesecake 94, 96
  Vegetable and Goat's Cheese Salad 36
chicken
  Braised Turmeric Chicken 44
  Chicken and French Bean Salad 142
  Chicken Kebabs 113
  Chicken Salad with Roasted Garlic 80
  Cold Marinated Breast of Chicken and Vegetables 184
  Creamy Glazed Chicken Legs 82
  Honey Chicken Thighs 44
  Lime Chicken with Mushrooms 132
  Lime-flavoured Chicken and Noodle Soup 124
  Mango and Chicken Soup 143
  Roasted Sesame Chicken 114
  Spicy Mushroom and Chicken Soup 56
  Stuffed Chicken Breast Wrapped in Parma Ham 149
  Tropical Mango Chicken 43
Chicken and French Bean Salad 142
Chicken Kebabs 113
Chicken Salad with Roasted Garlic 80
chicken stock 190, 191
Chicken with Cinnamon Sauce 92
Chilled Crab and Cucumber Soup 124
chillies 51–3
Chocolate Sauce 194
chutney 169
cinnamon 84–7
Cinnamon and Fig Gratin 97, 98
coconut
  Banana Crumble with Passion Fruit and Coconut 30
  Creamed Coconut and Pumpkin Soup 40
  Ginger and Coconut Tart 187
  Pumpkin and Coconut Cake 100
  Santen Seafood Salad 120
Cod Steak with Tomato Salsa 156
Cold Marinated Breast of Chicken and Vegetables 184
coriander 140–1
crab
  Chilled Crab and Cucumber Soup 109
  Potted Salmon and Crab 109
Creamed Coconut and Pumpkin Soup 40
Creamy Glazed Chicken Legs 82
Curry Sauce for Fish 193

D
Deep-fried Vegetables with a Guacamole Dip 121
desserts *see also* cakes and gâteaux
  Apricot Crumble 50
  Baked Gingered Apples 187

Index

Banana Crumble with Passion Fruit and Coconut 30
Cardamom-flavoured Peach Gratin 30
Chocolate Sauce 194
Cinnamon and Fig Gratin 97
Peach and Mascarpone Mousse 136
Poached Pear with Cinnamon 100
Raspberry Sauce 194
Ricotta Cheesecake 96
Sticky Banana Pudding 186
dressing
    salads 36
dressings
    for Broccoli and Cauliflower Timbale 76
    salad 22
Dublin Bay Prawn Broth 81
Duck with Banana and Orange Sauce 157

F

fish
    Cardamom Rice with Chicken and Fish 25
    Salmon Eastern-style 23
fish and seafood
    Aubergine and Smoked Mackerel 42
    Barbecued Monkfish and Prawns with Aubergines and Plum Tomatoes 77
    Chilled Crab and Cucumber Soup 124
    Cod Steak with Tomato Salsa 156
    Curry Sauce for Fish 193
    Dublin Bay Prawn Broth 81
    Fillet of Sea Bream with Shiitake Mushrooms 61
    Fillets of Sole with Roasted Peppers 125
    Gingered Prawn and Melon Salad 184
    Gratinated Coriander Mussels 157
    Grilled Tuna Steak with a Virgin Olive Oil and Garlic Sauce 126
    Lime-crusted Fillet of Brill 127
    Mackerel with Peri-Peri Sauce 132
    Monkfish with Beansprouts and Mangetout 91
    Mussel and Salmon Soup 37
    Oriental Cucumber and Salmon Salad 56
    Potted Salmon and Crab 109
    Prawn and Salmon Soup 164
    Prawn and Sweetcorn Chilli 57
    Prawns and Okra with Coriander 157
    Red Lentil and Clam Soup 89
    Red Mullet and Eel Terrine 180
    Red Mullet and Monkfish Stew 156
    Red Mullet Escabeche with Samphire 109
    Red Mullet with Black Beans and Mashed Potatoes 73
    Salmon and Pomelo Parcel 145
    Salmon in Lotus Leaves 108
    Salmon Roulade Served with Soya Beansprouts 185
    Salmon Steak with Celery and Cashew Nuts 81
    Seafood Salad 120
    Scallop Salad, Oriental-style 72
    Scallops and Prawns with a Glazed Potato Crown 168
    Sea Bass with Chinese Greens and Bacon 112
    Sea Bass with Indian Spices 41
    Sea Bream Served on Aubergine Purée 148
    Sea Bream with Asparagus in a Lime Sauce 133
    Shiitake and Smoked Haddock Soup 143
    Smoked Halibut Salad 165
    Smoked Mackerel Gratin 127
    Steamed Red Snapper 181
    stock 190
    Warm Salmon Timbale with Asparagus 144
fish stock 190

G

ginger 176-7
Ginger and Coconut Tart 187
Gingered Prawn and Melon Salad 184
glaces 192
Gratinated Coriander Mussels 157
Guacamole Dip 121
guinea fowl
    Roast Guinea Fowl with Kumquat Sauce 28
    Roast Marinated Guinea Fowl 64
    Tangy Guinea Fowl with Sweetcorn Chutney 169

H

Honey Chicken Thighs 44

L

lamb
    Lamb and Okra Hotpot 90
    Lamb Casserole with Stem Ginger and Cashew Nuts 186
    Lamb Chops with Limed Apricot Confit 128
    Loin of Lamb Wrapped in a Mousse of Coriander and Bread Croutons 153
    Medallions of Lamb with a Turmeric Crust 45
    Peppers Filled with Minced Lamb 48
    stock 192
    Tomato Bredie 90
Lamb and Okra Hotpot 90
Lamb Casserole with Stem Ginger and Cashew Nuts 186
Lamb Chops with Limed Apricot Confit 128
Lamb with a Turmeric Crust 45
lemon grass 160-3
Lime Chicken with Mushrooms 132
Lime-flavoured Chicken and Noodle Soup *122*, 124
Lime-crusted Fillet of Brill 127
limes 116-17
Loin of Lamb Wrapped in a Mousse of Coriander and Bread Croutons 153
Loin of Rabbit and Braised Lentils *170*

M

mackerel
    Aubergine and Smoked Mackerel 42
    Mackerel with Peri-Peri Sauce 132
    Oven-baked Aubergine and Smoked Mackerel 42
    Smoked Mackerel Gratin 127
Mackerel with Peri-Peri Sauce 132
Mango and Chicken Soup 143
Mango Gâteau 29
mangoes
    Mango gâteau 123
    Tropical Mango Chicken 43
mangoes
    Mango and Chicken Soup 143
Marinated Guinea Fowl 64

Mashed Potatoes 193
Medallions of Lamb with a Turmeric Crust 46
Melon Soup with Tapioca and Mint 21
Monkfish and Prawns with Aubergines and Plum Tomatoes 77, *78*
Monkfish with Beansprouts and Mangetout 91
mousses
    Loin of Lamb Wrapped in a Coriander Mousse 153
    Peach and Mascarpone Mousse *134*, 136
    Three-Pepper Mousse 60
Mushroom and Chicken Soup 56
mushrooms
    Fillet of Sea Bream with Shiitake Mushrooms 61
    Lime Chicken with Mushrooms 132
    Shiitake and Smoked Haddock Soup 143
    Spicy Mushroom and Chicken Soup 56
Mussel and Salmon Soup 37, *38*
mussels
    Gratinated Coriander Mussels 157
    Mussel and Salmon Soup 37

O

Old-fashioned Pork Stroganoff 64
Orange Sauce 194
Oriental Cucumber and Salmon Salad 56

P

pasta
    Piquant Pasta 57
pastry
    cases 20
    shortcrust 195
    sweet 195
Peach and Mascarpone Mousse *134*, 136
peaches
    Cardamom-flavoured Peach Gratin 30
    Peach and Mascarpone Mousse 136
peppers
    Fillets of Sole with Roasted Peppers 125
    Peppers Filled with Minced Lamb 48
    Red Pepper and Sweetcorn Soup 21

Three-Pepper Mousse 60
Peppers Filled with Minced Lamb 48
Pheasant with Apple and Papaya 93
pies and tarts
    Caramelized Onion and Cottage Cheese Tart 20
    Ginger and Coconut Tart 187
    pastry 195
    pastry cases 20
Piquant Pasta 57, *58*
Poached Pear with Cinnamon 100
pork
    Ham and Papaya Salad 165
    Medallions of Pork in Lime Sauce 129
    Old-fashioned Pork Stroganoff 64
    Pork Steak with Glazed Goat's Cheese 152
Pork in Lime Sauce 129, *130*
Pork Steak with Glazed Goat's Cheese 152
potatoes
    mashed 193
    roast 194
    Scallops and Prawns with a Glazed Potato Crown 168
    sweet 45
    Sweet Potato and Coriander Soup 142
Potted Salmon and Crab 109
poultry and game birds
    Braised Turmeric Chicken 44
    brown chicken stock 191
    Cardamom Rice with Chicken and Fish 25
    Chicken and French Bean Salad 142
    Chicken Kebabs 113
    chicken stock 190
    Chicken with Cinnamon Sauce 92
    Cold Marinated Breast of Chicken and Vegetables 184
    Creamy Glazed Chicken Legs 82
    Honey Chicken Thighs 44
    Lime Chicken with Mushrooms 132
    Lime-flavoured Chicken and Noodle Soup 124
    Mango and Chicken Soup 143
    Roast Duck with Banana and Orange Sauce 157
    Roast Guinea Fowl with Kumquat Sauce 28
    Roast Marinated Guinea Fowl 64
    Roast Pheasant with Apple and Papaya 93

Roast Quail with Nectarines 24
Roasted Sesame Chicken 114
Stuffed Chicken Breast Wrapped in Parma Ham 149
Tangy Guinea Fowl with Sweetcorn Chutney 169
Tropical Mango Chicken 43
Prawn and Salmon Soup 164
Prawn and Sweetcorn Chilli 57
prawns
    Barbecued Monkfish and Prawns with Aubergines and Plum Tomatoes 77
    Dublin Bay Prawn Broth 81
    Gingered Prawn and Melon Salad 184
    Prawn and Salmon Soup 164
    Prawn and Sweetcorn Chilli 57
    Prawns and Okra with Coriander 157
    Scallops and Prawns with a Glazed Potato Crown 168
Prawns and Okra with Coriander 157
pumpkin
    Creamed Coconut and Pumpkin Soup 40
    Pumpkin and Cashew Nut Cake 49
    Pumpkin and Coconut Cake 100
Pumpkin and Cashew Nut Cake 49
Pumpkin and Coconut Cake 100

Q

Quail with Nectarines 24

R

Rabbit and Braised Lentils 172
Raspberry Sauce 194
Red Lentil and Clam Soup 89
Red Mullet and Eel Terrine *178*, 180
Red Mullet and Monkfish Stew 156
Red Mullet Escabeche with Samphire 109
Red Mullet with Black Beans and Mashed Potatoes 73, *74*
Red Pepper and Sweetcorn Soup 21
rice
    Cardamom Rice with Chicken and Fish 25
    Mamdouh's Rice 189
Ricotta Cheesecake 94, 96
Roast Guinea Fowl with Kumquat Sauce 28
Roast Potatoes 194

S

saffron 32
salads
    Chicken and French Bean Salad 142
    Chicken Salad with Roasted Garlic 80
    Crunchy Vegetable and Goat's Cheese Salad 36
    Gingered Prawn and Melon Salad 184
    Ham and Papaya Salad 165
    Santen Seafood Salad 120
    Scallop Salad, Oriental-style 72
    Smoked Halibut Salad 165
    Vegetable Salad with Warm Tofu 22
salmon
    Baked Salmon in Lotus Leaves 108
    Mussel and Salmon Soup 37
    Oriental Cucumber and Salmon Salad 56
    Potted Salmon with Crab 109
    Prawn and Salmon Soup 164
    Salmon and Pomelo Parcel 145
    Salmon Eastern-style 23
    Salmon Roulade Served with Soya Beansprouts 185
    Salmon Steak with Celery and Cashew Nuts 81
    Warm Salmon Timable with Asparagus 144
Salmon Eastern-style 23
Salmon in Lotus Leaves *106*, 108
Salmon Roulade Served with Soya Beansprouts 185
Salmon Steak with Celery and Cashew Nuts 81
Salmon Timbale with Asparagus 144
samphire
    Red Mullet Escabeche with Samphire 109
Santen Seafood Salad 120
Sauce Anglaise 195
sauces
    Banana and Orange 157
    Black Bean Sauce 190
    Black Olive 61
    Chocolate Sauce 194
    Cinnamon 92
    Curry Sauce for Fish 193
    for Chicken Kebabs 113
    Horseradish Relish 82
    Kumquat 28
    Lime 129, 133
    Orange Sauce 194
    Peri-Peri 132
    Raspberry Sauce 194
    Sauce Anglaise 195
    Sweet Potato 45
    Tomato Salsa 156
    Virgin Olive Oil and Garlic 126
Scallop Salad, Oriental-style *70*, 72
Scallops and Prawns with a Glazed Potato Crown 168
Sea Bass with Chinese Greens and Bacon *110*, 112
Sea Bass with Indian Spices 41
Sea Bream Served on Aubergine Purée 148
Sea Bream with Asparagus in a Lime Sauce 133
Sea Bream with Shiitake Mushrooms 61
Sesame Chicken 114
sesame oil 104–5
Shiitake and Smoked Haddock Soup 143
Shortcrust Pastry 195
Sirloin Steak with Black Olive Sauce 61, *62*
Sirloin Steak with Horseradish Relish 82
Smoked Halibut Salad 165, *166*
Smoked Mackerel gratin 127
Sole with Roasted Peppers 125
soups
    Aubergine Soup 40
    Celeriac and Chestnut Soup 88
    Chilled Crab and Cucumber Soup 124
    Creamed Coconut and Pumpkin Soup 40
    Dublin Bay Prawn Broth 81
    Mango and Chicken Soup 143
    Melon Soup with Tapioca and Mint 21
    Mushroom and Chicken Soup 56
    Mussel and Salmon Soup 37
    Prawn and Salmon Soup 164
    Red Pepper and Sweetcorn Soup 21
    Shiitake and Smoked Haddock Soup 143
    stocks 190–3
    Sweet Potato and Coriander Soup 142
soy sauce 66–71
Steak with Sweet Potato Sauce 45
Steamed Red Snapper 181, *182*
Stem Ginger and Pear Cake 188
Sticky Banana Pudding 186

stock
    brown chicken 191
    brown veal 191
    chicken 190
    fish 190
    lamb 192
    vegetable 193
Stuffed Chicken Breast Wrapped in Parma Ham 149, *150*
Sweet Pastry 195
Sweet Potato and Coriander Soup 142
sweetcorn
    Prawn and Sweetcorn Chilli 57
    Sweetcorn Soup 21
    Tangy Guinea Fowl with Sweetcorn Chutney 169

T

Tangy Guinea Fowl with Sweetcorn Chutney 169
terrines
    Red Mullet and Eel Terrine 180
    Three-Pepper Mousse 60
tofu
    Vegetable Salad with Warm Tofu 22
Tomato Bredie 90
Tropical Mango Chicken 43
Tuna Steak with a Virgin Olive Oil and Garlic Sauce 126
turmeric 31–3
Turmeric Chicken 44

V

Vanilla Sponge 195
Veal Glace 192
veal stock 191
Vegetable and Goat's Cheese Salad 36
Vegetable Salad with Warm Tofu 22
vegetable stock 193

Page numbers in italics refer to illustrations

Conversion Tables

All these are approximate conversions, which have been rounded up or down. In a few recipes it has been necessary to modify them, so please always follow the amounts listed in each recipe. Also, never mix metric and imperial in the same recipe – this may affect the final result.

Oven Temperatures

Gas mark	°F	°C
1	275	140
2	300	150
3	325	170
4	350	180
5	375	190
6	400	200
7	425	220
8	450	230
9	475	240

Weight

Metric	Imperial
15 g	½ oz
25 g	1 oz
50 g	2 oz
75 g	3 oz
100–125 g	4 oz
150 g	5 oz
175 g	6 oz
200 g	7 oz
225 g	8 oz (½ lb)
250 g	9 oz
275 g	10 oz
300 g	11 oz
325–350 g	12 oz
375 g	13 oz
400 g	14 oz
425 g	15 oz
450 g	16 oz (1 lb)
500 g	17 ½ oz (½ kg)
1 kg	2.2 lb
1.5 kg	3.3 lb
2 kg	4.4 lb

Volume

Metric	Imperial	British	American
25 ml	1 fl oz		
50 ml	2 fl oz		
75 ml	3 fl oz		
100 ml	4 fl oz		¼ cup
150 ml	5 fl oz	¼ pt	
200 ml	7 fl oz		
250 ml	8 fl oz		1 cup
300 ml	10 fl oz	½ pt	
350 ml	12 fl oz		
400 ml	14 fl oz		
450 ml	15 fl oz	¾ pt	
500 ml	16 fl oz		2 cups (1 us pt)
600 ml	20 fl oz	1 pt	
750 ml	25 fl oz	1 ¼ pt	3 cups
900 ml	30 fl oz	1 ½ pt	
1 litre	35 fl oz	1 ¾ pt	1 qt

Length

Metric	Imperial
3 mm	⅛ in
5 mm	¼ in
10 mm (1 cm)	½ in
2 cm	¾ in
2.5 cm	1 in
3 cm	1 ¼ in
4 cm	1 ½ in
4.5 cm	1 ¾ in
5 cm	2 in
10 cm	4 in
20.5 cm	8 in
30.5 cm	12 in (1 ft)
91.5 cm	36 in (1 yd)
100 cm (1 m)	39 in

Spoons (Measured Level)

Metric	Imperial
1.25 ml	¼ tsp
2.5 ml	½ tsp
5 ml	1 tsp
15 ml	1 tbsp

All eggs are size 3 (extra large eggs) unless otherwise noted